With best wishes
To Don + Susie
David + Vera Mace

Oct 1983
Washington. D.C.

LOVE
&
ANGER
IN MARRIAGE

LOVE & ANGER IN MARRIAGE

DAVID MACE

Zondervan Publishing House
of The Zondervan Corporation
Grand Rapids, Michigan

LOVE AND ANGER IN MARRIAGE
© 1982 by The Zondervan Corporation
Grand Rapids, Michigan

LIBRARY OF CONGRESS CATALOGING IN PUBLICATION DATA
Mace, David Robert.
Love & anger in marriage.
Bibliography: p.
1. Marriage. 2. Anger. 3. Love. I. Title.
II. Title: Love and anger in marriage.
HQ728.M19   306.8'1   82-4776
ISBN 0-310-45290-2   AACR2

Edited by Penelope J. Stokes and Judith E. Markham
Designed by Kim Koning

Printed in the United States of America

82 83 84 85 86 87 88 / 10 9 8 7 6 5 4 3 2

To all married couples
across the world
who have together
made their commitment
to seek continuing growth
toward a creative, loving relationship

Contents

Preface

The Blue Dolphin Restaurant in San Leandro, Calif. has been the scene of numerous memorable gatherings, but none perhaps quite so unforgettable as the wedding reception that took place in mid-June. As the 300 guests chatted happily among themselves, they suddenly grew silent when the newlyweds began arguing in loud voices. Dismay turned to disbelief when the groom grabbed the wedding cake and threw it in his bride's face. By the time a police squad pulled up, guests were breaking chairs and smashing mirrors. It took half an hour for more than 30 police to get the crowd under control. By that time the newlyweds had disappeared.

This news item appeared in the *Britannica Book of the Year* for 1980, in a section entitled "Unusual But Noteworthy Events." Certainly an outburst of anger occurring so early in a marriage, in such violent form and so public a setting, may be regarded as "unusual." But if anger in marriage is considered "noteworthy," it is time we came to terms with reality and began to face the fact that love and anger go together much more frequently than our idealized romantic tradition has allowed us to acknowledge.

While recent studies of family violence have confronted us with some of the distressing results of misused anger in close relationships, for example, the "battering" of spouses, this is nothing new in human history. It has simply been an aspect of modern marriage that we have concealed and largely ignored.

However, this book is not directly concerned with family violence. Rather, I want to go behind the battering to the emotion of anger which motivates it and try to demonstrate that anger is not of itself evil, but only causes trouble and distress when it is misunderstood and misused.

During a lifetime of working as a professional in the field of marriage and the family, I have eagerly sought to understand the immense complexity of close interpersonal relationships. And I have often asked myself whether there might be one key issue that would explain why so many marriages, embarked upon with such high hopes, finally falter and fail. In time an answer began to emerge. First in my own marriage, and then in the marriages of many other couples whom I sought to help, the management of anger seemed to be especially important. As I continued to explore what I have called *the love-anger cycle*, I became convinced that I had tracked down the critical issue.

For several years I have wanted to write this book, but I always hesitated, feeling that I had not tested out my views thoroughly enough. As time passed, however, my conviction grew. Whenever I have written briefly on the subject, there has always been unusual interest on the part of readers. When I have spoken about it, I have always had an attentive hearing. When I have shared my ideas with couples, they have been very responsive. So, still with some hesitation, I have written the book. It may seem presumptuous that I should claim to see the relationship of love and anger more clearly than most other people do, but I *have* sometimes felt like that. If my perspective is anywhere out of focus, I stand ready to be corrected. But until then, I can only declare what I have come to believe, and what has stood the test in my own life and in the lives of others.

I am grateful to many colleagues and friends with whom I have had extensive discussions while I was seeking to clarify my ideas, and to many books, articles, and other materials I have read. Last, but not least, I want to thank the three typists—Connie Rhoads, Betty Huff, and Jill Beaver—who have shared the task of getting my thoughts down on paper in readable form.

PROLOGUE

Personally Speaking

An Autobiographical Statement

In writing this book I cannot separate the conclusions I have reached from a sequence of events in my own life. I introduce the autobiographical dimension immediately, so that you, the reader, will clearly understand the particular personal point of view from which I approach my task.

Vera and I are now in our forty-ninth year of marriage. We have actually lived together for only forty-six years, because the grim days of World War II separated us totally for just over three years. We would unhesitatingly rate our marriage as a happy one, and I believe our closest friends would concur in that judgment. As specialists in the field of marriage and the family, we have earnestly sought to "practice what we preach." We have greatly enjoyed our shared life and have found much fulfillment in working together in the service of others.

Yet as I now look back, I realize that in our earlier years of marriage the closeness of our relationship was far from what it has become in the later years. We were not aware of this at the time, because we did not then comprehend how much unappropriated potential we had. But by comparison with what we now enjoy, our marriage in the earlier years was relatively superficial.

Obviously, our understanding of marriage (despite the fact that we were "experts" in the field) has greatly improved, partially because of the gradual accumulation of experience and the natural process of adaptation to each other. But to a far greater degree, I believe it is the result of our deeper comprehension of the task of marriage, made possible by significant new insights from the behavioral sciences. This is particularly true in such areas as relational growth, the communication process, the creative use of conflict, and, above all, in a clearer understanding of the positive role that anger *can* play, yet seldom does, in close relationships.

So strongly am I now convinced of this that I would venture to make the following assertions:

1. The state of marriage generates in normal people more anger than they are likely to experience in any other type of relationship in which they habitually find themselves. Of course other relationships can and do generate considerable anger, but this usually leads to future avoidance of the relationship in question; or, if it cannot be avoided, it leads to the development of a protective "skin of indifference" which makes the relationship tolerable, even if it is not pleasant or rewarding.

2. Unless the anger thus generated can be processed as raw material for the development of intimacy, the possibility of closeness in the relationship is denied. The love and warmth that are sought in it fail to develop, and a sense of disillusionment results that can easily lead to alienation.

3. In society today we are witnessing this harmful process taking place on a tremendous scale. We see all around us the alienation of husbands and wives, of children and parents,

and of other relationships in and out of the family. The underlying cause of this widespread alienation is the fact that the persons concerned do not understand, and therefore are not able to process productively, the anger that is generated in their intimate interactions. The methods they use to deal with their anger are counter-productive.

4. It is possible, however, though not easy, to learn new skills which foster a more productive and creative use of anger so that it will reinforce, instead of destroying, love and intimacy.

Early Encounters With Anger

Vera and I recall very few occasions when we became angry with each other before we were married. Occasional frustration or irritation was not taken seriously at that time, because each of us believed that, once we were settled down in a shared life, we would come to understand each other better and have ample time and opportunity to straighten out any differences or disagreements that might arise between us. I believe this attitude is fairly characteristic of young lovers. The romantic glow creates an idealistic view of each other and a confident feeling that whatever may happen to couples in general, it will not be so in their case because they are special. This blissful state, I believe, makes the efficacy of premarital counseling questionable.

Once Vera and I got into the task of marriage, however, we began to realize that these exalted expectations were not going to be fulfilled. Looking back over such a long span of years, we don't trust our memories enough to reproduce particular anger situations in detail. But I can well remember the deep, painful sense of disillusionment which I experienced when I did in fact become very angry. Let me try to describe it.

I was aware of a rapidly developing state of tension. Somewhere in my chest, or down in the pit of my stomach, I felt a tangled knot that was giving me pain. There seemed to be a rapidly accumulating mass of hot, poisonous material some-where inside me. I was not conscious of any urge to attack Vera physically, but I was certainly clenching my fists and trying to keep myself under control. At the same time I was aware of a devastating sense of alienation and disillusionment because I was actually feeling hate toward the person I wanted, of all people in the world, to love.

My overwhelming urge was to disengage, to get away—out of Vera's presence—so that I could somehow deal with these frightening emotions which she seemed to be generating in me. My whole world seemed to be collapsing, and my impelling urge was to escape, to hide somewhere until I could begin to cope with the tumult within me.

This desire to escape dictated the policy I adopted at that time. Without explanation, I would make a hasty exit. Then, in isolation, I would try to calm my confused and heated emotions, striving to see the incident in clearer perspective and to balance it out with more positive feelings. As time passed, I would slowly calm down, get myself tidied up, and then return in the hope that our original good relationship could be restored.

Vera remembers that I was often gone for long periods of time. She had, of course, been made aware that something was wrong. Sometimes she could guess what it was, but often she had no idea what had happened to me. She concluded that I was a very "moody" person, and she had no idea how to respond to me. She wanted to talk with me about the situation, then or afterward, but she sensed that if she tried to do so, she would "rock the boat."

Her judgment was certainly correct. If she had tried to probe into the cause of my withdrawal, I would have responded negatively. Why? Because I feared that if we reactivated the issue that had caused my anger, the anger itself would also be reactivated, and I would be back where I had started. So, on the basis of an unspoken agreement, we put the situation behind us and proceeded as if it had never happened.

Thus, we were reconciled—but only until the next anger situation erupted.

I am reporting only my side of the picture. Vera is "slower to anger" than I am, but she *can* become very angry too. When she did, the "silent treatment" was her usual response.

We were not, however, willing to accept this situation. Although at that time we were unable to communicate directly about it, we were both unhappy and wanted to find a solution. This led me to a study of the psychological literature about hostility and aggression, which I'm afraid didn't prove very helpful. However, I did become convinced on one point. I learned that psychologically it is healthier to vent anger than to suppress it. (I still believe that to be true, though it can have dangerous implications.)

Anxious to find a solution, I decided to put this "venting" concept to the test. At first it was hard for me to stay with Vera and confront her, but I learned to do it. The inevitable result, of course, was that when I attacked Vera, she defended herself. And since the best form of defense can often be counterattack, we were soon getting into fights. As Vera puts it, "I waited till he was out of breath and then launched my offensive."

These were entirely verbal fights, but they were very painful to us both. One distinct advantage was that the issue was now out in the open, and we both knew exactly what was going on. Otherwise our arguments and hassles produced little in the way of positive results. The whole climate of our communication was so unpleasant that nothing was really settled. Vera sometimes cried, and that made me quite miserable and prevented any further communication about the issue. In the end we made up, and that was a pleasant relief, but little or nothing was accomplished in the way of improving our relationship.

Now we faced a crisis. It was clear that we would go on getting angry with each other from time to time; and it was equally clear that we had found no effective or constructive way to deal with our anger. This just didn't satisfy us. We believed there must be a better way.

Fortunately, by this time we were in the process of trying to improve our communication system. This made possible some calm, serious discussions about our inability to deal with our anger. And by way of further exploration, I had begun to study the *physiology* of anger—the bodily changes it brought about, and how these could be modified in certain circumstances.

Moving Toward a Solution

We now began to see anger in a more positive light. We recognized that it was a normal, healthy emotion which was evoked in certain circumstances and, when rightly responded to, could serve useful purposes. I realized that most of the psychological literature I had read was concerned with anger as a response to attack from a hostile source, a way of dealing with an enemy. But Vera and I were not enemies, and didn't want to be. We were friends and lovers, and anger between us seemed alien and out of place.

After much thought and discussion, we began to move toward a solution. Finally, after a good deal of experimentation, we devised an arrangement which, over the years, has proved highly effective. We called it our three-step plan.

Step One was an agreement that we would *communicate* our states of anger to each other as soon as possible, and hopefully before they could lead to unpleasant consequences. This was based on our conviction that anger was a healthy emotion which was trying to tell us something about ourselves and our relationship. We accepted as perfectly normal the fact that, in a close relationship, we would from time to time get angry with each other, and we gave each other full and free permission to do so. That really cleared the air and freed us from guilt.

We were greatly helped at this point by our understanding of the physiological dimension of anger, which I will discuss in detail later. We saw that it should be as natural to say to each other, "I'm angry," as to say, "I'm hungry," "I'm tired," or "I'm depressed." All are physical states.

Step Two was a pledge we made to each other that while it was O.K. to be angry, it was definitely *not* O.K. to attack the other in response to that anger. We saw that no gain of any kind could come from launching an attack. In fact, we used a vivid analogy which dramatized the situation for us: we made a contract that we would stop spitting at each other! We saw the venting of anger as a psychological equivalent of spitting, and we saw no justification for this between people trying to develop a loving relationship.

This agreement provided a valuable safeguard. If I knew that Vera was angry with me, but knew also that she would not attack (however much she felt the urge to do so), I had no need to develop retaliatory anger and launch a counter-attack. This provided a reasonable hope that we would not both be angry at the same time, so that normally one of us would remain calmly objective and in control of the situation.

While these two steps could be counted upon to keep us in communication and to prevent the possibility of fights, they were not of themselves enough. The anger, though now acknowledged and safeguarded from being vented, was still there. It was real, and painful, and demanded action. So something further was needed.

Step Three met this need. We made a contract that every anger situation that threatened our relationship would be *worked through by both of us* and *owned by both of us*, not as a personal weakness in the one who was angry, but *as a function of our total relationship*. In Step Three, the angry person requested help, and the one toward whom the anger was being directed gave assurance of a response.

The concept behind this was new to us, but of vital importance. It was a way of looking at anger which made our process work. I had often heard people say, "Your anger is yours,

and you must own it and take responsibility for it." I had even
heard it said that, "You make yourself angry—nothing and
nobody else is responsible." This concept, of course, led me to
withdraw from Vera, taking myself and my anger away and
trying to deal with it alone. But that didn't work—because it
was based on a misconception. While I alone have to deal with
my anger against the motorist who drove me off the road, or
the teacher who gave me a low grade, or the coach who drop-
ped me off the team, in a *close* relationship, the anger of either
against the other is a function of the total relationship and *can
be processed positively only by both acting together*.

So we adopted a policy that every anger situation between
us was in fact an opportunity for growth in our relationship
and must be dealt with accordingly—otherwise, we were
missing a valuable chance to achieve a deeper understanding
of ourselves and of each other. In other words, anger is not
something evil to be avoided or suppressed. It is not even
something inconvenient to be disposed of so that we can get
back to the business of living. It is, properly understood, *raw
material to be used* in the positive development of a better and
more secure relationship.

Anger is a secondary emotion—triggered by another emotion, deeper down. By getting back to the underlying primary
emotion and dealing with it, that particular source of anger
can be cleared up and removed.

When we sat down together after an anger situation and
processed our anger, Vera and I discovered that this was
always the case. And always we found either one of two situations. In the first, it turned out that I was angry with Vera for
something I *thought* she had said or done to me; but when we
really examined the situation, it became clear that I had misunderstood or misinterpreted the message I thought I received
from her. In the second situation, Vera was angry with me for
provoking her; and I had indeed, accidentally or intentionally,
pushed her beyond the limits of her tolerance. By working
through the situation, I began to understand how much toler-

ance Vera really had, and she learned what kinds of pressure pushed her over the edge.

Most importantly, we were steadily gaining confidence that we were now able to deal constructively with anger when it inevitably developed in our relationship. As time passed, we found that we had examined the major causes often enough to be familiar with them, so that if and when they recurred, we knew we could deal with them. And, of course, many of them stopped occurring, because we adjusted our behavior, and our interpretation of each other's behavior, so that the causes were finally removed.

We didn't expect that we would stop getting angry with each other. But since occasions for anger were being reduced and we were more confident now that we could cope constructively with anger when it *did* develop, our relationship was freed from any fear that anger could do us harm. This enabled us to take down defenses against each other that were no longer needed. Thus we became able to make ourselves vulnerable to each other without any fear of exploitation.

We have now come to understand that such vulnerability makes intimacy possible and removes the major hindrance to the growth of love in a close relationship.

Summing Up

This way of processing anger has made a marked and very welcome difference in the quality of our marriage. We don't say it is easy to do—it takes time and involves, at first, a good deal of work. But the rewards are tremendous.

Although we have not yet attempted to collect data of this kind on any systematic scale, we have evidence from other married couples that they have put these principles into practice and found them to be effective. And of course there may be other approaches that work equally well, or better, for some couples. All we claim is what we have personally experienced.

The primary test for us has been in our marriage, but we have also made ventures in using these procedures in other relationships. In any social relationship, if those concerned understand what is involved and are ready to make the necessary commitments to each other, the same good results should be possible.

PART 1

Understanding Anger

chapter 1

Body Language

The Physical Dimension

A well-known evangelist, in a brochure distributed in his meetings, declares in an arresting headline: "ANGER IS A SIN."

Most people, though they might not adopt such an extreme attitude, seem to believe that anger is a state of mind or, more precisely, of emotion that you produce in yourself, and for which you must take responsibility. In other words, you *make yourself angry* by a process that is under the control of the will. Moreover, this process is often considered to be an evil one. Although most people may never have considered this question seriously, when they do so they usually have to admit that this is the way they tend to think about anger.

Of course, many of the things people do when they are angry are indeed wicked, sinful, and very destructive. But so are many things which people do with knives, drugs, and automobiles, which are used by other people for good and worthy purposes. Even normal bodily processes like eating, drinking, and sex can be misused, with undesirable results.

What we need to understand, therefore, is just what anger,

as a part of our human make-up, is intended to do for us. I must confess that I had never considered this question until I began to study the subject seriously. When I *did* consider it, I came up with some surprising answers.

My major conclusion was that *anger is in fact our basic survival kit,* provided as a lifesaving resource when our very existence is threatened. Many simpler creatures use it for the same purposes we do.

I once watched a fly that wanted to get out of our kitchen to the wider world beyond. Starting out on this trip, it soon bumped against the window. This strange experience obviously took it by surprise. It could see the outside world very clearly, and there seemed to be no obstacle in its way. Yet there obviously *was* an obstacle. Bewildered, the fly walked with quickening pace across the pane of glass, expecting to be out in no time. But when this didn't happen, it obviously became agitated, buzzing and flapping its wings, and making a frantic effort to reach its goal. As far as I could judge by its actions, it was behaving exactly as I feel urged to do when I want and need something desperately but can't get it. The fly, I believe, was really angry. If the obstacle had been more flimsy—a spider's web, for example—its frantic efforts might have enabled the fly to break free before the spider got to it. In that case, the anger would have saved its life.

In the world of nature, most creatures are vulnerable to attack by roving predators. Small birds, for example, seldom sit still and relax on the branch of a tree. They fidget restlessly, looking this way and that, and are ready at the slightest sign of danger to fly away. They know that they would have little chance of fighting back if a prowling cat got within reach of them. The cat, in turn, if attacked by a dog, would arch its back, show its teeth and claws, make hissing sounds, and generally signal that the dog had better not attack for he might get the worst of it. If the dog were very large and very fierce, the cat might decide to adopt a different policy and bolt for the nearest tree.

Obviously these creatures undergo some kind of physical change when they become aware of danger or when they are frustrated. A remarkable series of bodily readjustments provides them with a sudden surge of energy which they can use either in self-defense or in retreat at the highest speed of which they are capable.

These bodily changes have been studied, and they are essentially the same for the fly, the bird, the cat, the dog—and for me when I get angry with Vera. They are part of a complex system of resources that become available when we are in a state of stress.

You and Your Emotions

Let us begin by recognizing that *anger is an emotion.* Before describing in detail how it functions in marriage, therefore, we ought to pause and ask: "What is an emotion? What causes it? How does it develop? How is it related to the way we think and to the way we behave?"

Emotions have now been extensively studied. Their basic function is *survival,* and they can be experienced at various levels of intensity. If I develop a negative feeling toward someone else, it can increase by stages from annoyance to anger, from anger to rage; similarly, I can move from apprehension to fear, from fear to terror.

In simpler creatures, emotions are generated by instincts. For example, an insect with a lifespan of only a few days does not have time to learn which creatures are friends and which are enemies. So, over a period of millions of years, the united experiences of its predecessors have been accumulated and passed down as part of its genetic inheritance. Something inside itself tells that insect where to go and where not to go and thus increases its chances of survival.

As living creatures become more complex, however, they become able to control their own behavior. Their brains become larger and larger, and more and more complex, right up to the very advanced human level. The human brain is reported to have as many as a hundred billion nerve cells (neurons), with connecting fibers packed in at the rate of ten thousand miles per cubic inch, and the neurons are sending signals back and forth at a rate that might reach one thousand impulses per second. Truly, as the psalmist says, "We are fearfully and wonderfully made."

Yet all that complexity has the same basic purpose as the brain of the insect whose lifespan covers only a hundred hours. The real difference lies in the fact that humans can *think*. By a process called *cognition* we can remember the past and we can guess at the future. Yet our fundamental emotions of fear and anger remain very much the same as those of the fly crawling on the windowpane.

In the task of understanding human behavior, careful studies of babies have taught us a great deal. The newlyborn infant reacts to the world it has entered with "undifferentiated excitement"; but soon these feelings divide into those that signal distress—fear, anger, disgust—and those that signal delight—elation, affection, and joy. In the average child, this differentiation has happened by the time it is two years old.

However, the negative feelings come first. A newborn babe can demonstrate anger, and often does. Birth has been aptly described as a "trauma," and it is very likely that in the womb the unborn child has already had to cope with some frustrating experiences. Because survival is the primary purpose of emotions, fear and anger are familiar experiences to us long before we learn to love. Some people don't learn to love until quite late in life—some not at all.

Fear and anger, therefore, are our basic emotions. Responsible for survival, they have been called "preparedness states." Anger is concerned with aggressiveness and attack, fear with defense and retreat. In the human infant, these cannot be distinguished at first. Both provide the necessary energy to meet unknown threatening situations. As the child develops, however, it learns to separate one from the other.

Fear is at first, for the baby, the experience of being confronted with a situation with which it is unable, or unwilling, to cope. Any sudden shock—a loud noise or a bright light—may produce a "startle pattern." The baby reacts with panic—loud screaming or complete paralysis. Later, when it becomes physically active, its reaction is to run away. Behind these outwardly observed behaviors, complex bodily changes are taking place. These changes continue throughout life. (The principle of the lie detector is that emotional disturbance can be identified by unseen changes in the body and the brain.)

Anger is also aroused when the child wants to respond to an instinctive drive to do something and then finds it blocked. We call this *frustration*. The baby's early responses are to kick, to stamp, to strike something—or to hold its breath. As it grows older, these undirected outbursts focus on attacking what it identifies as the cause of its frustration. This impulse remains in the person throughout life. That is what the word "anger" means.

How Anger Develops

It used to be thought that our various emotions were associated with particular body organs—you "loved with all your heart"; you "had no stomach for a fight." We now know that the *brain* is the controlling mechanism for all emotions, although other bodily organs can of course influence our feelings through the brain—especially the glands that produce hormones. On the other hand, our emotional states, like fear and anger, while they originate in the brain, greatly influence other bodily functions. This is especially true of anger.

What happens when you get angry? Let's try to list the various stages:

1. In your world, something occurs that becomes a negative stimulus. It is a threat of some kind. We sometimes call it a stressor. It has a disturbing effect on your equanimity. Usually it comes from outside, but it could be from inside your body such as a sudden stab of pain.

2. You become *aware* of this threat through one or more of your five senses. It could have started as a positive stimulus, but somewhere in your brain it got registered as negative, and this rings a kind of alarm bell.

3. When the alarm bell rings, your brain's response is a state of *anxiety*. This is a generalized emotional reaction to any negative stimulus, the precise nature of which has not yet been identified.

4. Stimulated by the alarm bell, your body has already gone immediately into *action*. In order to summon a surge of energy for whatever action may prove to be necessary, the appropriate section of your brain has called for immediate changes in your heart rate, blood pressure, and other body systems.

5. Now, and only now, your conscious mind gets into the act. It makes a *cognitive appraisal* of the situation and decides what should be done. At this point you, as a thinking, reasoning person, take control.

6. You *act*. The first behavior response may in fact be automatic, based on instinct, or on a previously learned behavior pattern which you have planned or practiced. But now you are in charge, and you are responsible for what happens next, and for the outcome of the incident.

This may not be a precise description of what happens in every anger situation, but it is useful for us to recognize the complexity of the events that are involved. Of course, most of them occur very rapidly—far more quickly than they can be described. For that reason, we can easily arrive at inaccurate conclusions about what our emotions are doing to us and about how we are responding to them.

New Studies of Behavior

All these processes have been extensively studied by physiologists and psychologists. At first, researchers had to judge what was happening to people by observing their facial expressions and body movements and by asking them questions. But fairly recent developments in the exploration of the brain have opened up a new and exciting chapter. It is now possible to manipulate animal behavior, and even human behavior, by applying electrical charges to the precise region of the brain that is in control. This, of course, opens the door to greatly increased understanding of the complex processes involved.

Physiologist K. E. Moyer's writings have been particularly helpful. By way of example, he describes

> a mild-mannered female patient who became aggressive, verbally hostile, and threatened to strike the experimenter when she was electrically stimulated in the region of the amygdala. When the current was turned off, she again became mild-mannered and apologetic for her behavior. Her hostile feelings and aggressive behavior could be turned on and off at the flick of a switch.[1]

While electrical stimulation brings about those anger reactions, chemical changes also are involved.

> Different hostility circuits are sensitized or desensitized as a function of certain blood constituents, particularly, though not exclusively, the hormones. It has been known for centuries that the raging bull can be converted into the gentle steer by lowering its androgen level through castration. This finding has been verified experimentally in a variety of animals.[2]

What we are concerned with here, however, is how neuron circuits in the brain are stimulated, not by experimental intervention, but by influences in the lives of normal individuals. Moyer explains:

> Certain hostility circuits appear to be sensitized by particular hormone balances and when these circuits are sensitized, a vari-

ety of environmental conditions will evoke hostile feelings and behavior. These environmental situations may involve frustration, stress in many forms, pain, or, if these circuits are highly sensitized, simply the presence of an attackable entity.[3]

These brief quotations sum up, in the words of a distinquished specialist in the field, what we need to know about the physiological basis of anger. A grasp of these basis facts leaves us in no doubt at all that the onset of anger is *not volitional*. To me, this is a profoundly important fact. When a state of anger is called for, a complex series of body changes occurs with astonishing speed, changes well-summarized in the June, 1979, issue of *Changing Times*:

> Consider the caveman. The sight of an enemy or dangerous animal sets off a series of hormonal and physical reactions. Adrenaline pours into his blood, speeding up his heartbeat and raising his blood pressure. Available fuel entering the blood as sugar increases, the red cells flood his bloodstream to transport more oxygen to the muscles and brain. Breathing accelerates to supply additional oxygen and to eliminate carbon dioxide created by sudden activity. Blood ordinarily required for digestion is shunted to the brain and muscles. Digestion slows. Pupils dilate, improving vision. Blood clotting ability accelerates, preparing for the possibility of a wound. All this gears the caveman for action to protect himself. In this aroused state he can stay and fight if the odds look good or flee if they don't.
>
> Our bodies react the same way, though the danger is more likely to be a letter from the IRS than a saber-toothed tiger. And the threat doesn't have to be immediate to cause arousal. Merely anticipate anything unpleasant, perplexing or uncertain, and you can feel the stress reaction go off inside.[4]

This remarkable process is an *automatic* response to a danger alert coming through one or more of our five senses, and it is transmitted immediately and directly to the appropriate sensitized region of the brain. There would be no time for this alert to be processed by the rational faculties of the highly developed human mind.

Do We Make Ourselves Angry?

In light of all this information, how do we answer such questions as: "Do we make ourselves angry?" "If so, just how do we do it?" "How far, therefore, are we directly responsible for being angry?"

Just try to put yourself in a state of anger. It proves to be very difficult, doesn't it? In fact, I can't do it at all except by deliberately focusing my attention on some situation that is very frustrating to me or some person who is treating me badly. But this means that the source of anger is there already, actually or potentially, and all I am doing is conjuring it up so as to produce a response in myself. I am able to do this because I am endowed with a memory and an imagination.

Could a fly do this? I greatly doubt it. So far as I am aware, simple creatures respond only to whatever is happening to them in the present. It is true that they have instincts to warn them of possible danger, but these are built-in components of their brains, not reasoning from memories of the past. Certain signals from the outside world produce an instant stimulus that means "danger," and the almost instant response to those signals is readiness for fight or flight. The same process occurs in me—except that the signals are much more complex and have been learned from my life experiences. For example, if a certain individual I meet from time to time produces danger signals in me, it doesn't mean that this happened the first time I met him; rather I have learned from later experience that he is out to get me, and the very sight of him represents a danger signal.

Suppose I am traveling along a jungle trail in an Indian forest and suddenly see a tiger ahead. Do I say to myself, "That's a tiger. It may or may not be a man-eater. I wonder if this is a dangerous situation?" Long before I could entertain such a train of thought, something in me much more primitive than reason would send a wave of fear through me and instantaneously start the series of complex body changes. This would happen far more swiftly than my conscious mind could direct or control it. There is no time for deliberative processes. If I had to rely on them, it might be too late.

I repeat, the onset of anger is an immediate response to a stimulus that comes to me through one or more of my five senses. The rapidity with which this happens is impressive. In terms of its physical components, the anger is there before my conscious mind can recognize and record it. My body tells me I am angry and then hands over to my mind the responsibility for deciding what to do. By the time I am aware of anger, the process of providing the extra surge of energy necessary to deal with it is already well advanced.

Striking confirmation of this fact comes from Paul Ekman, professor of psychology at the University of California Medical School. He is an expert on the human face and has developed the Facial Action Coding System, which registers the role of facial muscles in expressing human emotions.

Ekman explains that narrowing of the lips is one of the earliest signs of anger. In particular, Muscle 23, a certain facial muscle, can provide an enlightened observer with reliable information about the onset of anger. The tightening of this muscle "often betrays the person's feelings before he or she becomes aware of them."[5]

What this tells me is that *I am never directly responsible for being in a state of anger*. I am responsible only for what I do with my anger after my conscious mind has taken over. Therefore, it cannot be said that anger is sinful. Anger can be used to commit sin, to be sure, but that is an entirely different matter.

My anger response may in fact turn out to be a false alarm. Someone who looks at a distance like a deadly enemy may, as he comes nearer, be recognized as a cherished friend. The ghost in my bedroom may, after all, be no more than the window curtain billowing in the night breeze. The seemingly hostile expression on my wife's face may be her unconscious response to a sudden twinge of pain.

Anger, therefore, is a spontaneous response, below the level of the conscious mind, to a danger signal, real or imagined. At the incipient stage it is entirely outside my control. I am not responsible for it, but only for how I respond to it.

Ways of Responding to Anger

What kinds of responses are available to me when I become aware that I am angry and that the energy for action has already been provided by my body? There are four possible responses:

1. *Fight*. As soon as I become aware that I am being attacked, I have to make a vital decision. Is my opponent powerful enough to defeat me in combat, or do I have a good chance of achieving the victory? I may, in fact, not have any options—I may be caught in a situation where escape is impossible; or my opponent may be able to command more speed than I could, so that if I run he will catch up with me when I have exhausted a good part of my store of precious energy. There may be no alternative but to stand and fight.

As we are all aware, the art of fighting is not just a matter of brute strength. With skill, I can defeat an opponent who is stronger than I am. So even if my conscious mind played no part in my becoming angry, it must now be vitally involved in developing a sound strategy. Unless I fight with cunning, I may squander my precious resource of energy and lose the battle.

Anger prepares me for the fight. The tension in my muscles makes them ready for action. So getting into a fight is a very natural and obvious response to anger. My opponent means to hurt me or has already done so. Now it's my turn to launch an attack on him, to strike where he is most vulnerable—tit for tat, an eye for an eye, a tooth for a tooth. In all of us there is implanted a certain exaltation when once we are really aroused in self-defense. We say "our blood is up." We find an elemental sense of fulfillment in battering an enemy and a vicarious excitement and joy in watching others fight. Something deeply implanted in us responds to the summons to battle—something powerful enough to overcome our fear. Courage, as we call it, is a quality greatly admired.

Animals generally fight seriously only under certain conditions—when they need food, during mating season when competing for the females, and when attacked. Young animals fight as a form of play, but they are careful not to hurt each other. Animals of the same species seldom fight to kill each other and do not normally continue to attack a rival who has admitted defeat. The human race, alas, is distinctive in having carried fighting to an extreme point in terms of wars and massacres. Government records show extremely high rates of violent crime in the United States, and recent reports on family violence reach appallingly high figures.

2. *Flight*. When threatened by attack in a dangerous situation, I may judge at once that my chances of defeating my adversary are not good and that it would be better to try to get away. Discretion, it is said, is the better part of valor, and wisdom may often dictate escape from the danger situation as the prudent policy.

However, the choice between fight and flight can be a difficult decision if fighting is a real alternative. If I fight and defeat my opponent, he will probably not attack me again, because he knows his chances of victory to be poor; whereas if I run away, he may only bide his time and then attack again.

It might even be best to fight until the odds become clearer and then switch to flight if it seems I will be defeated. As the old rhyme says:

> *He who fights and runs away,*
> *Will live to fight another day.*

If flight is clearly the solution, I need to have a sound policy. Where can I go, if hotly pursued, to find a secure refuge? How can I be sure that I will not land in a dead end or run into an accomplice of my adversary? Flight may require as much skill and good judgment as fighting.

3. *Freeze*. There are some small creatures who, under at-

tack, have little chance either of overcoming their adversary or of getting away. Their situation appears hopeless. In these circumstances, they may "play dead," lying perfectly still and showing no sign of activity. This policy seems a desperate stratagem, yet is does pay off at times. The predator may not notice them and may pass by without awareness of their presence. Or, the attacker may assume that they are already dead and not worth killing—anger dies down quickly if there's nothing to be angry at.

The muscular control needed to freeze goes contrary to the purpose of anger, which is to give a surplus of energy for action. Yet if freezing is the only option, it obviously makes sense; and for poorly protected creatures this must have developed as an instinct which best served their purpose. The important point is that *anger can, under appropriate circumstances, be totally controlled,* despite the fact that it tends naturally to issue in vigorous action.

4. *Relax.* Anger, as we have seen, is a state of bodily tension caused by involvement in a stress-producing situation. The demands on the body's resources are considerable because a prodigal output of energy may be required, an output justified in order to survive the crisis.

However, the body is not comfortable in a state of tension. Accelerated beating and heightened blood pressure are exhausting to the heart. Tense muscles tire quickly. Normal functions like digestion may be temporarily suspended or upset. A state of anger is a state of emergency, and the body is eager to return to normal functioning. If this doesn't happen within a reasonable period of time, a condition of complete exhaustion may ensue.

While the body is eager to be relieved as soon as the emergency is past, it is unable to determine when this happy condition has been reached. Like the civil defense services when the air-raid sirens sound, the body leaps into action and must remain on alert until it receives the "all clear" signal. That signal must come from your conscious mind, because only your best judgment can determine when the danger is past and the situation has returned to normal.

This signal can be given under two conditions. The first is when the fight is over, the flight has reached a point where there is no further danger, or the predator has gone away so that there is no further need to remain motionless. In other words, when all danger is past, the body systems can return to normal functioning and take a period for rest and recovery.

The second is when the danger signal was a false alarm. What looked or sounded or felt like an attack was really an entirely harmless event, and no state of emergency is called for. As we have seen, it is important to respond instantly to every possible indication of danger, before the conscious mind has time to assess the situation. But when that assessment has been made, and there is in fact no danger, the mind signals the body that it may now reverse the state of preparedness and go into relaxation. Until that signal has been given, the body must remain in a state of tension.

Many people make a mistaken judgment about anger. When aroused, they say that they must "express" their anger in order to "get it out of their system." Actually, this is saying to the body: "Keep the anger coming—the fight (or flight) is still on." Of course, vigorously exerting tense muscles brings at least physical relief to an angry person, but that is something different from "expressing" anger. As David H. Burns, a psychiatrist at the University of Pennsylvania Medical School, points out, "Treatment strategies that urge the patient to 'get the anger out' by expressing aggressive feelings are rarely, if ever, effective."[6]

So venting anger by beating pillows only relaxes the tense muscles. Such action may feel good, but it doesn't deal with the anger. Probably it would be more effective to let all muscles relax and hang loose, and that would also communicate to the body the unmistakable message that the crisis had passed.

(Incidentally, it is my conclusion that the term "expressing anger" is a very confusing one and should be abandoned. It has two separate and quite different meanings. It may mean communicating the fact that you are in a state of anger—a very important matter for married couples—or it may mean acting on your anger in one way or another. It is generally taken to mean attacking the object of your anger, but in my judgment, "venting anger" expresses this much more clearly and is not subject to confusion and misunderstanding.)

Anger can be responded to in any one of these four ways, all of which are under our control. The body presents us with the resources to meet a crisis; the mind must then take over and decide how to act. All four options would normally be open, or two or more of them could be used in sequence. We are not, however, responsible for *being* angry, but only for how we *respond to* and *use* anger when it is already there.

In this chapter I have tried to summarize briefly the physiological facts about anger. Without this knowledge about the way our bodies function, we simply cannot understand what is happening to us in close relationships. The lack of this vital information has led to a great deal of needless misery. It was therefore essential to focus on this material in our opening chapter.

chapter 2

Hostile Aggression

The Social Dimension

So far we have considered anger only as a response to being attacked. That is, of course, a very narrow view. Yet it is a good way of getting into the subject, because it gives us a relatively simple and clear picture of anger as a series of body changes for which we are not responsible, but to which we have to respond in one way or another.

However, we must now look at the other side of the picture and consider the viewpoint of *the attacker*. Obviously the one who makes the attack is also angry and needs an abundant supply of energy when the fight or the chase begins. But he is not responding to being attacked, so the instigating stimulus for him is not danger, or threat, or fear. Is the physiological process therefore different in his case?

Apparently not. The body changes seem to be the same. There is, however, a different and more complex process at work in getting the changes started.

The attacker is not responding to an alarm bell set off by a wave of *fear*. Instead, the bodily changes can be brought about by a variety of emotional states. And the response is not defensive, but offensive. In fact, it is customary to describe it as *hostility* or *aggression* — or *hostile aggression* — rather than anger.

The aggressive drive is complex. In fact, different kinds of aggressive behavior are controlled by different areas of the brain. J. P. Flynn, a physiologist quoted by Moyer, carried out an experiment that illustrates this vividly.

> The work coming out of Dr. Flynn's laboratory has shown that if a very friendly cat is stimulated in the lateral hypothalamus through an implanted electrode, it will ignore the experimenter and attack an available rat. However, if the cat is stimulated in the medial hypothalamus, the cat will ignore the rat and attack the experimenter.[1]

This experiment demonstrates that there are different kinds of aggressive behavior, each having its own special stimulus and each triggering a different physiological mechanism. Moyer goes on to classify the known forms of aggression, emphasizing the fact that this is a new field of investigation and much still remains to be learned about it. At the time of his writing, seven different forms of aggression had been identified:

(1) *Predatory Aggression*. Here we are dealing with creatures that survive by hunting and devouring other creatures. Hunger sets up frustration, and the search begins for a meal. Catching sight of the prey greatly intensifies the aggressive urge, and the chase is on. Man also can be a predator: hunting and fishing are common forms of "sport," and in some communities the captured prey provides food necessary for survival.

(2) *Inter-male Aggression*. This is described as a "relatively unique" form that is often associated with sexual jealousy. One male identifies other males, particularly intruding strangers, as rivals seeking to mate with the available females. We certainly find the counterpart of this in our human communities, and it is sometimes a disturbing factor in a marriage.

(3) *Fear-induced Aggression*. This describes the situation where an animal is attacked, or thinks it is going to be attacked, and responds by itself becoming an attacker. This form of aggression must by definition always involve an attempt to escape before the attack is made. The idea is that the animal doesn't really *want* to fight, and its first urge is to get away; but if its escape is blocked, then it will launch an attack on its attacker. This is obviously the kind of situation described in detail in the last chapter. Most husband-wife quarrels begin when the attacker is attacked in return.

(4) *Irritable Aggression*. In this case, a state of anger or rage has already developed, usually as a result of frustration or pain. This produces an urge to "lash out" at some person, animal, or even inanimate object, which is perceived as the cause of the trouble. This is the most common cause of anger in close relationships like marriage.

(5) *Territorial Defense*. This form of aggression has been extensively described by such writers as Konrad Lorenz and Robert Ardrey in books that have become best sellers. Many animals and birds stake out a territory which they regard as their exclusive property, and any other creature is regarded as an intruder to be attacked and driven away. However, the urge to attack quickly subsides once the intruder moves out of the forbidden area, and there is normally no further pursuit. We are all familiar with this kind of aggressiveness at the human level, from "Keep Out" signs erected on the borders of private property to marriage partners who stake out either space or time which each wants to preserve for his or her exclusive use.

(6) *Maternal Aggression*. This exclusively female form of aggression is found in most mammals and in birds. A mother with young will fiercely attack any intruder judged to be threatening. As the young develop and become independent, however, the mother's urge to attack dies away.

(7) *Sex-related Aggression*. Situations that stir sexual desire sometimes also stimulate aggressive tendencies. The mating

process often includes, symbolically if not realistically, the pursuit of the female by the male. Such aggression is seen in an extreme form in the high incidence of rape in our modern communities.

The Controversy About Human Aggression

These seven forms of aggression, identified in animals, reflect the *competitive* nature of life in what has been called the "wild kingdom." Because there isn't "enough of everything for everyone," the business of living becomes an endless stuggle for supremacy. Nature, as Tennyson expressed it in his poem "In Memoriam," is "red in tooth and claw," and the law of the jungle is "the survival of the fittest."

Does this then mean that brutality is the principle that governs life in the jungle? Some have said so, but others have disagreed. I have already referred to the writings of Konrad Lorenz, who studied intensively the aggressive impulses of animals and came to the conclusion that "aggression is primarily *not* a reaction to outside stimuli, but a 'built-in' inner-excitation that seeks for release and will find expression regardless of how adequate the outer stimulus is."[2] Lorenz goes even further and asserts that aggressiveness brings important *benefits*—it makes life a struggle, and by so doing contributes to the survival of the species.

The views of Lorenz apply, of course, to human beings as well as to animals. Indeed, it appears that humanity is worse than the animals, because humans kill members of their own species with a ruthlessness that seems to enjoy cruelty for its own sake.

The opposite side of the argument is represented by Ashley Montagu, who declares, "All of man's natural inclinations are toward the development of goodness. . . . There is not a shred of evidence that man is born with 'hostile' or 'evil' impulses which must be watched and disciplined."[3]

It is not my purpose here to take sides in this age-old argument. But we must face reality; we live in a world in which good and evil are both present, and within us all there is a potential for aggressive behavior which can have destructive consequences.

All the known forms of aggressive behavior have been carefully investigated. The studies have confirmed, beyond any question, the physiological basis of anger. However, ways are now being found of controlling such impluses, not only in animals, but also in human beings.

In the last chapter I gave an instance of aggressiveness being stimulated by electrical impulse. Here is an account of the opposite process:

> Dr. Heath, in New Orleans, reports that he has implanted permanent electrodes in the septal region of violent psychotics. The patient can then be brought into the clinic, paranoid, raging, violent and threatening. He is plugged in and stimulated, having no awareness of the stimulation. His response is immediate. He relaxes, his hostility dissipates, he smiles and is at peace with the world. It is a short step from here to give the patient his own transistorized power pack with an anti-hostility button that he himself can press whenever he feels his intolerable hostility coming on. The technical problems have already been solved.[4]

Also, quite apart from the use of drugs and electrical impulses, the evidence now suggests that "aggressive response tendencies can be modified by learning. . . . The individual can be taught to inhibit aggressive responses."[5] Later we shall see some ways in which this can be done for married couples.

Toward a Definition of Anger

Obviously aggression and anger are related, but what is the difference, if any? A definition of anger, though heretofore avoided, is now important, because I believe that at least part of our difficulty in understanding anger is due to confusion about what the word really means.

The English language contains a rich and wide variety of terms reflecting various concepts about anger.

The first is *heat*. Anger is viewed as a state in which the body is on fire. We talk of "red-hot anger," of "blazing anger," of being "inflamed," in a "fiery temper," or "seething with anger." We "see red," are "hot under the collar," "incensed," or "boiling mad."

A second concept is *hostility*. An angry man is "malicious" or full of "animosity" or "acrimony." He is in a state of "indignation," "irritation," or "resentment," full of "fury" and "ire." He will "storm" or "rage," implying the threat of violence. Like an animal, he may "growl" or "snap" or "gnash his teeth."

The third concept is *violent action*, anger vented or about to be vented. The angry person is "hopping mad." The analogy of volcanic upheaval is also used—he will "fume" or "erupt" or "blow his top." He will be "convulsed with anger," will "storm with rage," "fly into a rage," be "violently angry," or "in a frenzy." He will "throw a tantrum."

Sometimes the emphasis is not on aggressive action, but on a *sour state of mind*. Such an angry person may be "sullen" or "morose." He may "sulk" or "scowl" or give you "black looks." He will "bridle" or "bristle," "pout" or "glower." He is "piqued," "takes offense," or "takes umbrage."

Finally, the angry person is seen as *being in a state of ill-health*. Physically, he is full of "bile" or "choler." Mentally, he is "in a bad temper," "has lost his temper," or is "in a stew." He is "out of his mind" and cannot be approached or reasoned with as a normal person. Indeed, an angry person is viewed as not being entirely responsible for his actions. One of the most common terms we use is "mad."

This is an impressive vocabulary of negative terminology. Is it any wonder that we have totally overlooked the positive functions of anger and have denounced it ruthlessly as an unmitigated evil? The tragic consequences of this become very clear when we try to deal with anger in close, intimate relationships—like marriage.

The *American Heritage Dictionary* says that anger is "a feeling of extreme displeasure, hostility, indignation, or exasperation toward someone, or something." I personally cannot accept this definition, for the word "extreme" limits the condition to an excessive degree of anger; whereas I know I can be mildly angry and yet be genuinely angry. This tendency to think of anger only in its extreme forms is common, as we have just seen.

In *Funk and Wagnalls* (1931 edition), I found two different definitions. The first was, "violent, vindictive passion; sudden and strong displeasure." Here again the emphasis is on extreme feelings only. However, the second definition was, "trouble; anguish; distress." That sounds more accurate. After all, you can always add adjectives if you feel that your particular anger is unusually extreme, strong, or violent.

Next, I went back to linguistic sources and reaped a rich harvest. I was familiar with the German word *angst*, which appears in our English word *anxiety* and has much the same meaning. In Old English the prefix *ang* means something sharp and painful, like a spike. In Old Norse the word *angr* means "grief," which is experienced like a sharp pain. The Latin word *angere* means "to strangle or draw tight," which again suggests what anxiety and grief feel like. Another Latin word, *angustus*, means "narrow," similarly suggesting a feeling of tightness. Finally, the Greek *ankhein* means "to squeeze," and *ankhone* refers to "strangling," the source of our English word *angina*, the chest pain suffered in a heart attack.

As often happens, our modern usage has given the word anger an extreme and derogatory connotation. Originally the emphasis was on the distress and discomfort the angry person suffered, not on the urge to respond with a violent attack on the person presumed to be the cause.

The baby comes into the world with undifferentiated feelings. It knows only that at certain times it is relaxed and feels pleasure, while at other times it is uncomfortable and feels displeasure. In the first state the child is content and has no urge to take action. In the second state, it wants something changed and tries to do something about it.

For the purpose of my discussion, therefore, I propose a very simple definition of anger:

Anger is any feeling of displeasure directed against a person (or object), accompanied by a desire to remove the cause.

This definition delivers us from the need to indicate the intensity of the feeling—anger can be strong or weak. It covers the gamut, from a simple request like, "Please speak louder so I can hear you," to a raging fury which attacks another person with intent to murder. Between husband and wife, it can cover everything from a mild pinch to a knockdown, drag-out fight.

Anger is basically self-assertion. It is the defense system of the *ego*. Just as the body needs a defense system to protect it from attack by micro-organisms which try to invade it, so the ego, the personality, the self needs a defense system. When the ego is attacked or invaded, a warning system goes into action and generates anger.

Anger says, "Look, I'm here, and I have needs. I have sensitivities that can be hurt. I have rights that must be recognized. I have a point of view that needs to be heard. Please be sure that you don't ignore me or brush me aside or ride roughshod over my territory. If you do, you must expect me to assert myself and to do so vigorously, or even violently, if necessary."

If you have a well-balanced sense of who you are and what your rights are, you will be guided by your anger in a threatening situation to take the appropriate action. Some people, though, will overreact and use their anger explosively and destructively. Other people will underreact and fail to assert themselves when they need to do so; they can be helped by what we call "assertiveness training."

Anger in Close Relationships

Broadly speaking, two emotions provide the motivating force for anger in a close relationship. Anger begins with an attack of some kind—intentional or unintentional. Let us suppose that the husband launches the attack. The emotion prodding him will almost certainly be *frustration*—he feels displeasure and wants something in the relationship to be changed, to his advantage. The desire for change may be so mild that it takes the form of a polite request. No anger may be experienced at this stage. But there is always the potential for an attack, which will appear very clearly if the request is refused in a way which can be interpreted as unreasonable rejection—a put-down.

If the wife interprets her husband's request as unreasonable, or inappropriate, or ill-timed, she senses danger and experiences the emotion of *fear*. She is aware that this situation may be difficult to handle. If she mismanages it, she may bring on a crisis in the relationship, and she wants to avoid this. However, mingled with her fear may also be frustration. She is annoyed because her husband has made this advance at this particular time, or annoyed because he has made it at all. If her frustration is stronger than her fear, she may respond sharply and launch an attack which will intensify the husband's feeling of frustration and, as he considers where this may lead them, generate some fear for him also.

For both of them, therefore, the exchange, sparked by frustration or fear or both, results in some discomfort and even pain. The anger, as always, is a secondary emotion, generated by primary emotions that are the real causes of what is happening between them. If they were not seeking a close relationship to each other, the anger might be used as *power*, to give one of them supremacy over the other; or it could put *distance* between them, so that their negative feelings toward each other would cease to seem important. If, however, they wish to continue in a close relationship, the only way is to process the anger by dealing together with the causes of the fear and frustration that triggered it.

While most of the seven forms of aggression can play a part in starting a marriage crisis, the motivating emotions, again and again, are *fear* and *frustration*. These cause pain in the form of hurt feelings, which in turn generate anger. As a rule, frustration plays the initiating role, while fear and hurt feelings may follow as responses.

Marriage Causes Frustration

Marriage brings frustration because it is based on the concept of a shared life. Two people, who have up to that point lived separately, now decide to live together. Instead of acting independently, owning property and planning time and making decisions individually, they now pool their resources and adopt a system of joint ownership, planning, and decision-making. Marriage means, inevitably a sharp reduction in the dimensions of their living space. They choose togetherness, but in the process they inevitably give up a large amount of separateness.

Studies of animals have demonstrated that when space for living together is reduced, significant changes take place in behavior patterns. The same happens for human beings: irritation, confusion, restlessness, and aggressiveness emerge as individuals try to cope with the space limitations.

If you were to increase the space taken up by the fixtures and furniture in your house or apartment, you would find it harder to move about. You would have to pick your way carefully; your activities would be slowed down; you would have to work harder to perform accustomed tasks; and you would increase your chances of bumping into obstacles, doing damage and hurting yourself.

If as well as increasing the number of objects in your house, you also doubled the number of people, you would by the same process increase the number of activities to be performed and perhaps also the amount of time needed to do them. All these changes complicate the nature and the number of operations to be performed so that the needs of each person could be met, instead of the needs of only one person.

Of course, ideally in marriage all this should be compensated for by the pleasure of enjoying the company of your partner. At least, that is the theory behind getting married. But it simply stands to reason that there will be times when the *complications* appear to be so exasperating that the *compensations* hardly seem worth it. At these moments, feelings of frustration lead to a state of irritability, which makes you angry. Your beloved partner now becomes an obstacle, blocking your progress, upsetting your emotional balance, getting in your way, and hurting your feelings. The perfectly natural result of frustrations of this kind is that cooperation turns into competition, good will into ill will, and friendliness into anger.

Such frustration can happen in the best of circumstances, in a situation where there are few outside pressures or demands to complicate the flow of events. However, this is not the setting in which most married couples live today. On the contrary, frustration is ever-present in our contemporary culture, placing us in situations where irritation is continually assailing us. Just look at the many changes that have come about since the beginning of the century:

1. *Life is much more complex.* In the so-called "good old days" you would probably have lived out your life in the community where you were born; at most you would have made only one or two moves. Beyond that, major travel would have been a rare and exceptional event. You would have married and settled down, probably staying in the job for which you were first qualified, with little change apart from possible promotion. Your circle of friends would likewise have remained fairly constant, and with them you would have shared your spare-time interests and hobbies. Your knowledge of the outside world would have come from reading the local newspaper and an occasional book or magazine. Music and entertainment would have been provided by a few phonograph records, an occasional silent movie, or a local concert. The idea of a sea voyage, an airplane flight, a visit to a foreign land, even a radio or TV program, would have sounded like a wildly im-

possible dream. You would not have experienced these things either because you had never heard of them or because they seemed completely out of your reach. Yet all these new and exciting possibilities are real options today for most of us. These alternatives are pleasant, but also put pressures on us that make us want to do everything, to go everywhere, and to meet everyone who sounds interesting.

2. *Standards of social and personal behavior are no longer uniform.* Communities in earlier times were generally made up of like-minded people, and departures from traditional practices were frowned upon; the risks of departing from them were just too great to be seriously considered. The influence of public opinion was too powerful to be challenged, so people generally conformed to the accepted practices in the way they dressed, behaved socially, and conducted their family life. Failure to conform to the accepted behavioral norms could lead to rejection and isolation that might mean the end of everything they cherished. Consequently, married couples generally found it best to meet community expectations, and so to avoid trouble.

3. *The tyranny of time pressures is demanding and often exhausting.* In the past, because your options were limited, you had a reasonable amount of what was called "free time." And it was fairly easy, unless you lived below the poverty line, to employ someone to clean your house, tidy up your yard, or wash and wax your car (or feed the horse and clean the buggy). Nowadays, most of us have to do these and other routine jobs ourselves. Besides, in order to keep up our standard of living and cope with inflation, we have to work long hours, or maintain a two-income marriage, or go in for a bit of moonlighting. In addition, there are special movies or TV programs we don't want to miss, books we want to read, committees we ought to attend, areas of work that seem never to get cleared up, letters to write, bills to pay, local or visiting friends with whom to "get together," courses in further education we want to take—not to mention the ever-present need to vacuum the house and tidy up the yard and clear out the garage.

In a word, the schedules many people are trying to maintain today are positively awesome. As a result, many of us are under almost constant strain, short of sleep, and living on the edge of chronic irritability. Under these conditions, our relationships—and especially our close relationships—are really suffering. It takes only a hurtful incident or remark occurring in the family to cause us to explode in frustration and anger. And when that happens, the whole series of interconnected associations in our lives could begin to collapse like a row of stacked dominoes.

4. *Competitiveness in marriage is encouraged by today's new values.* In the marriages of the past, cooperation was established by the acceptance of gender roles for husband and wife, which kept them out of each other's clearly defined "spheres of influence." In the home, husbands did the outside jobs, wives the inside jobs. The husband was the breadwinner, the wife the homemaker. In the event of a possible conflict of interest, the husband had the right to make the final decision, which the wife generally accepted without question.

Today, by contrast, the two-vote system is widely accepted, which inevitably leads to long discussions and painful arguments before decisions are finally arrived at. Today, in more than half of all marriages the wife is gainfully employed outside the home, and the husband's roles often include household chores and parenting responsibilities. Time pressures make "gracious living" virtually impossible, and children often spend long periods of time under outside supervision or left to their own devices. Individual rights and personal assertiveness are stressed in today's values, making the clash of wills between husband and wife a frequent possibility.

Frustration, frustration, frustration. It's a strange payoff for the rich dower of technological marvels and labor-saving devices that have fallen into our laps in the wealthiest and most developed culture in the whole span of human history!

A Case in Point

To illustrate the point as dramatically as possible, and to demonstrate our human fallibility, let me share an incident which happened recently to Vera and myself.

We had returned from a series of programs in other communities and planned to relax and spend a few days in our mountain retreat. My part of the plan was to get on with the writing of this book.

After a two-and-a-half-hour drive, we unpacked the car, had an evening meal, and went to bed early. Next morning, full of high expectations, we woke at our usual hour. It is our practice to start every day with what we call our "sharing time"—getting in touch with each other's feelings, thoughts, hopes, and fears.

I began by relating a dream in which I had been leading some kind of seminar. I had done badly and had come under criticism. My self-esteem was deflated, and I felt inadequate.

Vera then shared some apprehension she had about someone who was coming to visit us. I had similar misgivings, but I criticized her for making over-elaborate plans. She found this hurtful and reminded me that she was only sharing her feelings. I realized that I had been negative, and apologized, explaining that I was very tired.

At breakfast, Vera asked me when I was taking the car to be fixed. This was the last thing I wanted to be reminded of, and I replied firmly that I wasn't taking it at all. I planned to work all day on my writing, and the car could wait. I said I felt she was nagging me. She replied that she only wanted to know when *she* could have the car and had no ulterior motive. I responded by saying I wished she could have made her message clearer, for I had completely misunderstood it. She bridled at this and said she thought I should have been able to understand what she meant.

Before we could clear this up, I had to make a phone call. As I finished dialing, somehow the connection was broken. I felt frustrated but kept on trying till I got through. All I had to do was give the man at the other end an address, but he launched into a long conversation about irrelevant matters. This was taking up my precious time, and I was paying for the long-distance call, so my irritability went up another notch.

I now went to the bathroom to clean my teeth, eager to get to work. As luck would have it, the cap of the toothpaste tube fell to the floor and rolled to an inaccessible place, so I had to get down on my hands and knees to retrieve it. I felt discredited, ill-treated, and—yes, frustrated.

Finally, nearly half an hour later than I had planned, I got to my desk and spread out my papers. You guessed it. I was now so exasperated that I couldn't concentrate on my writing. It took me another half-hour to process my accumulated feelings. Later, Vera and I put the record straight by agreeing that we had both been tired and irritable and had made too-heavy demands on ourselves and each other. We took some time off to relax, and then felt much better.

Does all this sound familiar? It illustrates what we mean by the social dimension of anger.

We need to be reminded that this exciting twentieth century, which has brought us so many privileges our forefathers never even dreamed of, has also greatly increased the complications with which we have to cope. The very fact that we have so many options to choose from, and are surrounded by so many comforts and conveniences to which we assume we are entitled, has widely extended the possibility of our becoming irritated and angry with those nearest and dearest to us. We must therefore learn to deal more effectively with these negative feelings when they arise.

chapter 3

Love Versus Anger

The Relational Dimension

Even attempting to see how love and anger confront each other in every close relationship, and what this does to the relationship, is difficult, because nearly everything that has so far been written about anger fails to treat it relationally or to see it positively as raw material for growth. The tendency is first to assume that you shouldn't feel angry toward a person you love, but if you *do*, you are having "problems" and you'd better not talk about it out loud. And if you must do something about it, you should either have a fight and then make up, or swallow your anger and hope it will go away. None of this is very helpful, as plenty of couples will testify. Fortunately, there is a better way.

Since we now have a definition of anger, we ought also to have a definition of love. Many books have been written on the subject, but I have neither the inclination nor the space to explore it here in depth. So I will content myself with the often-quoted statement attributed to psychiatrist Harry Stack Sullivan—"When my desire for the health and wellbeing of another person becomes equal to my desire for my own health and wellbeing, then the state of love exists."

Let's go back to the baby again. When it is born, its awareness hardly extends beyond its own body, and the only kind of love it can experience is self-love. However, as we have seen, it has probably already had some frustrating experiences of anger.

Birth is followed by a series of encounters with a new and unfamiliar environment which can furnish many causes for irritation. A baby peacefully asleep is a study in tranquility; but an infant who is hungry or uncomfortable provides a dramatic demonstration, in its reddened, contorted features, of anger and exasperation. It is a kind of undifferentiated aggressiveness, directed at nobody or nothing in particular.

As we begin life, therefore, we experience anger some time before we are able to feel love. Perhaps the goal of maturity is to learn more and more to reverse that order.

There are many theories about how we learn to love in the process of growing up—initially from self-love to object love, first directed to the mother, then to other family members, then to relatives, friends, and associates. With the onset of puberty, love directed to a possible mate becomes romantic love; then comes parental love for children, and, later, for grandchildren. We talk of altruistic love as the final goal, and Carl Rogers has coined the phrase "unconditional positive regard" to describe it.

Humans are without doubt gregarious creatures, and our need to share life with others is paramount. It is possible to live in a state of distance, even of partial alienation, from others, but something of vital importance usually gets lost in the process. For our full personal development, as well as for our achievement of a secure sense of personal identity, we need close, intimate relationships. I cannot be really secure in my sense of identity until I have experienced a continuing close relationship in which I am "fully known and deeply loved." Only then can I be sure, beyond any question of doubt, that I am really okay. And to be complete, this experience should be mutual within the relationship.

A close relationship is not a luxury. It is a basic need. The institution of marriage has been having a rough time in recent years, yet there is convincing evidence that married people generally are happier and healthier than the single or the divorced. This is true regardless of the very mixed quality of the marriages in our population. If the really happily married were separated out for comparison, my guess is that the contrast between them and the unmarried would be spectacular.

It is not surprising, therefore, that one of our primary goals in life is to achieve at least one really loving relationship; and those who fail to do this don't give up easily—the majority of divorced persons try again, and some of them yet again. In fact, one of the main reasons so many marriages are failing today is that our expectations of what marriage has to offer have risen so high that they have become unattainable for large numbers of people. Vera and I once wrote a book called *Marriage: East and West*, which was based on an extended comparison of married couples in the Orient and in Western society. Our main finding was that in East Asia people's expectations of marriage were comparatively low, and they were therefore usually satisfied with what they got; while in the West, people expected so much that most of them were inevitably doomed to be disappointed.

I am not, however, suggesting that high expectations of close relationships should be abandoned. If our expectations go beyond the reach of attainable reality, some scaling down is called for. But a really loving marriage is not unattainable. It is hard to get, but when you do get it, the rewards make all the efforts abundantly worthwhile.

G. K. Chesterton once said of Christianity that it had not been tried and found wanting, but rather had been found difficult and not tried. That could also be an accurate description of marriage, except that too many people have not known clearly what they were supposed to be trying to do and have, therefore, applied the thrust of their efforts in wrong directions and, consequently, failed. One purpose of this book is to help remove that kind of ignorance. (What I have said about marriage is, of course, true of other close relationships, including parent-child relationships.)

How a Love Relationship Develops

I believe that close relationships fail so dismally and so often because the quest for love leads to a series of frustrating experiences which produce so much anger that the love is destroyed and the quest is finally abandoned, whether or not this is outwardly acknowledged. Only when the anger can be dealt with and processed creatively can this disastrous situation be avoided. The majority of people fail to process anger in their close relationships because it is not only a difficult task, but also a task which is very poorly understood.

To help us understand, let's follow the fortunes of John and Mary, two young people moving into marriage, and watch the interaction process that takes place between them.

At some point John and Mary meet for the first time—as strangers. If it is a case of "love at first sight," they are attracted to each other right away. If not, they may simply become friends, and over time the friendship deepens into something more vital. Either way, the point comes at which they become aware that they perceive each other as very special and feel drawn together in a common quest for intimacy and lasting love. In cultural terms, this means that they agree to move toward marriage.

They now begin to spend a great deal of time together, getting to know each other better and exploring each other's personalities at a variety of levels. This is for the most part an exciting, highly pleasurable experience. They discover many common interests—enough to fortify their confidence that they are suited to each other as partners in a shared life. If this doesn't prove to be the case, they may have to break up—a painful but wise course to take in those circumstances.

The dominant motive as John and Mary deepen their relationship is the pull toward intimacy. Like love, intimacy has been analyzed and described in many books, but a simple definition—"shared privacy"—will suffice. Intimacy simply means opening up to another person areas of our personal lives which we normally conceal out of fear that airing these areas could make them vulnerable to attack. Mutual self-disclosure in a love relationship, therefore, is an authentic venture of trust that tests, and hopefully finally validates, the relationship. If we really love each other, we can prove it by sharing our personal secrets and, in so doing, enter into a special relationship that transcends all others. This is a significant step toward the final goal of being fully known and deeply loved, which confirms the identity of each as an authentic and lovable person. The process of self-disclosure should proceed slowly and mutually, but there is no substitute for it.

Somewhere along the way, as this process unfolds, the wedding takes place. It is important to understand that a wedding is not a marriage, although we tend to interchange the words without discrimination. The wedding is simply the outward social announcement that the two people, after testing out the promise they seem to hold for each other, are now ready to embark upon the task of building a marriage. Whether in the end they manage to do so remains to be seen. (Every year in the United States more than two million men and women go back to the state which registered their wedding and report that they have failed to achieve a marriage and now want the contract to be canceled.)

The Making of a Marriage

From the accumulation of all their past life experiences, John and Mary have brought a heap of raw materials. The wedding ceremony is an outward declaration to their relatives and friends that they are now raking these two separate piles of raw materials together into one pile and are ready to commit themselves to the task of rearranging these materials into a pattern of shared living that they hope will be happy and harmonious for both. In the wedding ceremony they are claiming the social and legal support that community and state provide as they establish a new unit of human society. The religious wedding ceremony means that they also claim the help of God, and of the religious community to which they belong, in the difficult task that lies before them. The full significance of these ceremonies is seldom referred to nowadays, but that is what a wedding really means—claiming in advance the support and help to which we are entitled from community and church.

When John and Mary rake the two heaps of raw materials together, they gradually identify and sort the various components. For all practical purposes, these fall into three distinct categories:

1. *Congruent Living Patterns*. In this pile we find all the habits, tastes, and preferences that John and Mary share. They both like Beethoven, pizza, tennis, chess, foreign travel, camping, working in the yard, picnics—the full list would hopefully be a very long one. These represent the activities and arrangements that can quickly and easily be built into their shared life. With these adjustments they should have no trouble.

2. *Complementary Living Patterns*. These represent differences in their habits and tastes, but of a kind that can fairly easily be adjusted. John is an intellectual and fond of scholarly discussion, an area in which Mary feels insecure; but she is eager to improve her mind, and John is ready to help her to do so. Mary is socially at ease in all kinds of gatherings, but John sometimes feels shy and awkward; he hopes, however, that Mary will give him support and guidance. In these and other areas and activities, they look forward to supporting and learning from each other.

3. *Clashing Living Patterns*. But there are areas in which tensions are sure to arise between them and in which difficult and painful adjustments will be necessary. For example, John is untidy with his clothes and other possessions, while Mary

keeps everything orderly and well-organized. Mary is an early riser and likes to get the day's activities well under way by breakfast time; John sits up late but is sluggish and sleepy in the morning. These are the areas in which they are going to frustrate each other until they can make behavior changes which will lead to mutually acceptable accommodations.

Their goal, remember, is intimacy—to share each other's lives closely. But as we have seen, close relationships inevitably mean coming together in limited space; and limited space is known to cause frustration.

Suppose I go to a meeting and happen to meet a man with whom I disagree about almost everything we discuss. When I get home, I tell Vera what an unpleasant person he was. Meanwhile, he is telling his wife how unpleasant I am! But no harm is done, because our lives are widely separated. If we happen again to go to the same meeting, we will simply avoid each other.

But supposing by chance we two men find ourselves employed in the same business. Then the chances of unpleasantness are much increased. And if the boss happens to put us together on the same assignment, we would be in serious trouble.

The principle is clear. Of course John and Mary get on well together; that's why they have chosen to marry. But don't forget that third category of raw materials—the differences between them which bring about a clash of wills. Inevitably, these are going to cause trouble. Mary's meticulous tidiness will clash with John's disorderly ways.

One day a crisis will arise. Let us suppose that Mary's parents are coming to stay with them for a week. Mary, naturally, tries to get the house clean and in good order. Things that John has left lying about are pushed out of sight. He can't find something and complains; but Mary firmly insists that she won't allow John to scatter his property about the house—particularly when her parents are there as guests. John responds by saying this is unreasonable—it's his home as much as hers; why can't he do what he likes in his own home? Some bad feelings are now being stirred up. Mary feels let-down and put-down. John stubbornly refuses to yield and says he wishes Mary's parents weren't coming. Mary feels outraged at this and declares that if John won't welcome her parents in their home, she won't ever invite his parents to visit. Both are now really angry with each other. Instead of loving each other, they are temporarily hating each other.

How Differences Lead to Conflicts

This is, of course, a typical situation, so it provides a good illustration or example of the three stages in the difference-to-conflict process:

1. *Difference*. John and Mary have different standards about tidiness. They always knew they had, but somehow until now the issue didn't come to a head—at least not on the present scale. The difference was loosely tolerated but not really faced.

2. *Disagreement*. A difference turns into a disagreement when the space becomes limited. Mary was annoyed before about John's untidiness, but she tried to overlook it—perhaps by picking up things for John and incorporating him in her space; perhaps by insisting on tidiness in her parts of the house, but turning a blind eye to places where John functioned. But now she is insisting on enlarging her space—when her parents come she wants the whole house to meet her standards—and reducing John's space by leaving him nowhere to be untidy. So the issue can no longer be side-stepped. John and Mary are forced to confront each other in open disagreement.

3. *Conflict*. A conflict is *a disagreement heated up*. A situation arises where the clash of wills can no longer be suppressed or avoided. John and Mary now confront each other in a power struggle, both angry and ready to attack each other. Right now, there is no feeling of love between them. It is impossible to feel loving and angry at the same time. Not that anger is the

opposite of love. It isn't. The opposite is cold, callous indifference. But the *feelings* of love and anger can't be experienced
together. One excludes the other.

Just now, anger is in charge. The danger signals between
them are triggering off on both sides that "surge of energy"
which prepares for fight or flight. They don't want intimacy
any more. They have become adversaries. Each wants either
to subdue the other or to make the other accept his or her
terms. If this is not possible, they want to get away from each
other, because each feels that his or her right to behave normally is being violated.

John and Mary now stand at the point of crisis. Either they
will resolve the conflict effectively and come back to each other
with their love warmly restored, or they will fail to resolve it
and begin to move away from each other. Their relationship
will either advance toward a higher level of intimacy, or it will
begin to slide downward toward degeneration and decay.

One incident alone will not have such far-reaching consequences, of course. But the way John and Mary deal with this
incident will probably determine how they continue to deal
with this particular difference between them, making it a re-
curring occasion for successive experiences of alienation or
intimacy, for these habit patterns are not going to disappear.
Also, their handling of this particular disagreement will likely
become the behavior pattern that will determine how they
handle later disagreements that will inevitably occur in their
relationship.

I call this critical process in a close relationship *the love-anger
cycle*. Drawn together by their desire for love and intimacy, the
couple try to share their lives in a process that inevitably
reduces the space in which each is free to move and act. As far
as their congruent and complementary living patterns are
concerned, this closeness is richly satisfying because in these
areas they support and reinforce each other. If all their living
patterns did this, they would have no conflicts.

But no two people ever will, or probably ever should, want

always to do the same thing in the same way at the same time. So differences are inevitable, and disagreements are inevitable. Conflicts are *not* inevitable, theoretically, because a disagreement *can* be resolved without anger. But this is not a part of normal human experience, because we are not perfect. Some conflicts are likely to occur, although over time they can with wise handling become less and less likely.

Most couples have conflicts. The anger that heated up the disagreement then temporarily destroys the love between the couple and forces them to take refuge in distance from each other. Thus separated, they cool down, the anger slowly dissolves, and in time love stirs again and they experience a renewal of their need for closeness. Then they resume the quest for intimacy which had been rudely discontinued, and for a time all is sweetness and light.

But inevitably, they drift into another disagreement and another conflict. The process of alienation recurs, and they take refuge in distance. So *the love-anger cycle repeats itself*, over and over, *in all close relationships*. These inevitable points of crisis for any two people who seek intimacy with each other are the decisive points at which the complexities of their needs for individual independence, dependence, and interdependence have to get sorted out.

chapter 4

Is Anger Sinful?

The Ethical-Spiritual Dimension

We have left John and Mary in a painful and distressing situation. They are facing each other as adversaries in a belligerent mood. Their fists are clenched, their faces hot and flushed, their eyes glaring defiance at each other. They are distressed, embarrassed, confused, perhaps ashamed. But their jaws are firmly set, and each is determined not to yield to the other.

Let me assure you that we shall rescue them in due course, but for now we must leave them undisturbed while we ponder another aspect of their predicament.

The title of this chapter asks a question: Is anger sinful? And behind that question is another question—not an easy one to answer: What is sin? Many books have been written on the subject, but again, we shall have to be satisfied with a short and simple definition.

Sin is a transgression of divine law; part of this transgression is using our power for action to do evil rather than to do good. But what is evil? It is whatever we do that thwarts the best possibilities that lie in any given situation, judged in terms of our own highest interests and the highest interests of others, taken together.

It would be easy enough, by this standard, to come to the conclusion that anger is sinful. We have all experienced, over and over again, the damaging and destructive things that can result from the actions of angry people. But because people often *do* sinful things when they are angry, does that inevitably mean that it is sinful to *be* angry?

We have seen that anger is a state of being highly energized, and that we can choose to act in a number of ways when we find ourselves in that particular state. Supposing we choose to process our anger in order to learn what we can do to change the situation for the better—to bring good out of what might have ended in evil. Is *that* sinful? Surely not.

You can't read the Bible without coming across many instances of anger. On a rough count, the word "anger" is used about a hundred and fifty times, and the word "wrath" another fifty times. In addition, there are other passages which refer to anger, although the actual word is not used. If you examine these passages, you will discover that in many of them, especially in the Old Testament, it is *God* who is angry. And in the New Testament, we are told of a time when Jesus became so angry with the merchants and moneychangers who were desecrating the temple that He overturned their tables and scattered their wares (John 2:13–17). On another occasion He is reported as being angry with the Pharisees (Mark 3:5). And in the Book of Revelation there are two references to "the wrath of the Lamb" (6:16–17), and others to the wrath of God.

Now if the Bible portrays God as being angry, how can we say that anger is sinful? Of course, God's anger was always directed against sinful behavior on the part of men and women. But if anger is sinful, that still means that God, by way of showing His disapproval of sin, resorted to sinful behavior Himself in order to do so. A statement like that simply doesn't make sense! So, in the light of what the Bible says, it is impossible to say that anger is sinful.

Since anger is given to us to fulfill a vital purpose—to protect us from danger and even to save our lives in a dire emergency—shall we say instead that *only vented anger is sinful*? No, even that would be an inaccurate statement. For if we look carefully at the Bible passages which describe God's anger, we shall find that He is not only *being* angry, but also *acting on* His anger. He is *venting* it. And that was certainly what Jesus was doing when He overturned the tables of the merchants and the moneychangers. He was using His anger to draw attention publicly to behavior that was inappropriate and irreverent in a holy place.

When Venting Anger Is Appropriate

So far I have suggested that the venting of anger represents undesirable behavior. However, I have been speaking only of anger in close, intimate relationships. On a wider scale, the venting of anger is often necessary, because it represents the only constructive action that can be taken.

Because human beings invariably live together in communities, and because the expectations and wishes of individuals are often in direct opposition to those of other individuals, some means must be found of maintaining social order. There are, in fact, two different systems which make it possible for a group of people to live peaceably together. The first system is based on authority and obedience. The second system is based on love and trust.

The authority-obedience system is very familiar to us. We find it operating almost everywhere—in the military system, in most community and business organizations, and in government. It operates just as often, though in simpler forms, in primitive tribes as in highly developed nations. For example, the Australian aborigines, though they wear practically no clothes and build no dwellings, have quite a complex social organization.

In order to survive, tribal groups have to unite. In an emergency they must close ranks and act together. Thus, a designated leader is appointed—almost always a man, and a person who can command allegiance. As chief of the tribe, he is in a position of authority; he has power to command and must be obeyed. The penalties for disobedience usually include being driven out of the tribe and losing the support of the group, a fate which is greatly feared. Because of the fear of rejection, the members of the tribe can be counted on to respond when the chief uses his authority. This principle guarantees social order. It is basically an appeal to self-interest, and an effective one.

Any unwillingness to respond to authority creates a crisis and usually brings an angry response from the chief. The anger is vented in the form of a threat, quickly followed by punishment, and the offender is brought into line. Anger is therefore a necessary dynamic for the maintenance of social order.

Some tribal chiefs misuse their power by acting unjustly, so there is a tendency for human communities to set up tribal councils, at which the elders get together in dealing with offenders. In time the punishments for particular offenses come to be defined, and customs that prove workable develop into codes of law with specified penalties.

All this is, of course, familiar to us, but I want to stress that *the dynamic behind it is anger*, creatively used to establish and maintain law and order. Because we all become angry with people who steal and kill, we turn our corporate anger against them and punish them.

Authority and Obedience in the Family

For most of human history, we have structured our families in much the same way. In earlier times, extended families were quite large, and they functioned very much like tribes, with the father playing the role of chief. In order to put the system of authority and obedience to work, we established what is sometimes called a "pecking order"—a man has authority over a woman, an older man or woman over a younger, an adult over a child. We call this the hierarchical family, from a Greek word which means "a body of persons organized according to rank, capacity, or authority."

This order led to good behavior in the family, as it does in the wider community. Children knew that if they made their parents angry, they would be in trouble. If the husband got angry at his wife, she had better toe the line and be submissive. In the family, as in the military, there was a "chain of command."

This pattern was the accepted norm in the biblical family, and consequently some people have called it the "Christian family" pattern. But, in fact, it is no more Christian than Jewish, or Muslim, or Hindu, or Buddhist. It was the universal pattern in all traditional families in the major human civilizations.

What has influenced many Bible readers is that Paul accepted the hierarchical pattern as appropriate for Christian families in his time. This is not at all surprising. Paul himself was not married. He was expecting the world to come to an end very soon and therefore considered that it would be best for Christians not to marry at all (1 Cor. 7:8). If, however, they were already married, naturally they should accept the social custom of their time. Paul's intention was not to lay down rigid rules for married couples living in a very different world nearly two thousand years later!

Paul writes some very beautiful things about marriage, of which we may well take heed, but as in other portions of scripture which include social custom, we need to separate spiritual truth from the local practices of Palestine at the beginning of the Christian Era. Christians today do not model their educational system, or their legal system, or their fashions, or their diets, or their architecture, or their home furnishings on the patterns in use in New Testament times.

Recognition of these differences is important because our

growth in Christian understanding may be involved. There is another quite different system for the management of relationships in human communities, and the time has come to examine it.

The Hebrews' understanding of their relationship to God was that He was the supreme authority to whom they must be obedient. They perceived Him not only as Creator, but also as King and Judge. Hebrew spiritual and ethical standards were far superior to those of surrounding tribes, and there was always a danger of apostasy. Because nothing short of rigid rule could maintain the purity of the faith, God was often seen as jealous and even vengeful. Consequently, He was portrayed as demanding obedience, and ready to use power to enforce it. This emphasis was strengthened because Israel was perceived as the chosen people, with a special mission to perform. Hebrew marriage and family life, therefore, reflecting the religious system, was also seen in terms of authority and obedience.

Nevertheless, many Old Testament passages portray God in a very different role—as a loving father, kind and merciful and forgiving. These passages can be seen as preparing the way for the message of Jesus, who preached the gospel of love and trust as the basis of the Christian community. For Jesus, God was, above all else, the loving heavenly Father who called His children to reflect in their own lives and relationships the love that was proclaimed and lived by His Son.

What Jesus Taught About Marriage

In terms of direct instruction, the teaching of Jesus had very little to say about the husband-wife relationship. It was not His custom to address the particular conventions of His time, but rather to lay down principles for living that could be applied to all human relationships. Yet preachers are often bewildered about what to say about Christian marriage, because New Testament material on the subject seems fragmentary and even confusing.

But when we take a rather different approach, a wealth of insight appears, and in at least three areas. First, all that Jesus said about loving relationships (sometimes about "you and your brother") has direct application to you and your spouse. Second, the rich and deep quality of His own personal relationships with others provides abundant examples of love in action. And third, the revolutionary attitude He adopted toward women stands out in stark contrast to the prevailing views of His time. Although a whole book could be written on this subject, a single example must suffice.

Jesus enshrined the Great Commandment as the heart of His whole message: "Love the Lord your God with all your heart and with all your soul and with all your mind and with all your strength. . . . Love your neighbor as yourself. There is no commandment greater than these" (Mark 12:30–31). It would hardly be possible to find language stronger and more authoritative.

At the human level, the key word is "neighbor," which means "the person nearest to me." And for any married person that is surely the marriage partner, the one chosen person who shares my life at its deepest and most intimate level. Of course, I have other "neighbors," but this interpretation seems to me the most clear and obvious one.

Now, if I love my marriage partner as I love myself, I cannot treat him or her either as a superior or as an inferior. For me, this basic, central teaching of Jesus moves marriage decisively into the sphere of a fully equal partnership. And in doing so, it fulfills an original promise in the second chapter of the Book of Genesis—that God gave Eve to Adam because Adam needed, above all else, *a companion*.

Bible Teaching About Anger in Marriage

If Jesus had anything significant to say about human relationships, it was that His message was intended to move human society from the system based on authority and obedience to the system based on love and trust. And that means to move progressively from using anger as a social restraint to using it as the raw material for relational growth toward mutual trust.

Jesus spoke some very pertinent words about anger in close relationships. Since they use the "brother" formula, I will take the liberty of changing that word in Matthew 5:23–25. Freely translated, the message would read: "If you are on your way to church and are aware that there is an unresolved anger situation between you and your wife—stop and turn back! Your first Christian duty is to clear up the conflict in your marriage; and then, and only then, are you ready to worship God." In other words, process your anger first, because your protestations of love for God are unacceptable if you are not on terms of open love and trust with those who are nearest and dearest to you. Can there be any doubt that this is what Jesus is saying? If doubt remains, put it to the test of experience.

Paul has something very similar to say in his letter to the Ephesians: "In your anger do not sin: Do not let the sun go down while you are still angry" (4:26). Interestingly, the passage accepts anger as normal and inevitable. Paul is saying is that Christians will inevitably be angry from time to time. However, they should be careful not to let their anger be vented in a destructive way, because they would then be sinning. The right thing to do is to clear up the anger situation as soon as possible, and preferably before going to bed that night.

We cannot leave this theme without a word about a great Christian concept, *forgiveness*.

The only part of the Lord's Prayer that touches on the subject of human relationships is the petition for forgiveness. Too often we rattle through the words of the prayer without stopping to realize what we are saying. What we *are* saying is that all the other things we are asking for in the prayer are free gifts to us from a loving God. But if we have sinned and wish to be free of our burden of guilt, there is a condition that must be met. We must first take action to clear up any state of alienation which may exist in our relationships with others

—whether the fault is ours or theirs. This is forcefully emphasized, both from the positive and the negative sides, in Matthew 6:14–15. And the same point, that our relationship with God and our relationship with others are integrally related, is stressed in the parable of the unforgiving servant in Matthew 18:23–35.

The Christian message is replete with material about the complexities of human relationships—sin, repentance, and forgiveness; anger, alienation, and reconciliation. As the English poet William Cowper has expressed it:

> *The humblest and the happiest pair*
> *Will find occasion to forbear;*
> *And something, every day they live*
> *To pity, and perhaps forgive.*

Strangely enough, however, few preachers seem to have given attention to the rich vein of teaching about Christian marriage that appears when we begin to insert "you and your spouse" in passages dealing in a more generalized way with human relationships.

Christian Marriage—Hierarchy or Companionship?

There is no doubt in my mind as to why the "chain of command" pattern became the basis for traditional marriage in all the major human cultures. The two-vote system, which otherwise seems ideal, can introduce so much disagreement, heated up by anger into conflict, that it makes stable, secure families difficult to achieve and to maintain. And since family stability has always been the foundation of social order, this was simply a risk that could not be taken.

A clearly defined authority figure, therefore, needed to be "in command" of every home. Thus decisions could be firmly and quickly made, even if they did not always represent the best policy. A one-vote system seemed essential.

Naturally, the headship of the home was awarded to the husband. In times when fighting prowess was the quality most needed for leadership, men were given the authority, and women were conditioned to be subservient. This plan didn't always work smoothly, but it turned out to be the best available; and over long centuries it became thoroughly established. The price that was paid, however, was that the personhood of women was often denied and even debased.

Given the apparent necessity for one-vote marriages, the only system that was workable was the one based on authority and obedience. Love was simply not given any serious consideration, either in choosing marriage partners or in defining the marriage relationship. Only duty mattered, and the duty of the couple was to produce children and to carry on the family traditions into another generation. Given that, the quality of the relationship was of little importance.

Only in recent centuries, with the advent of democracy, has the picture changed, and changed radically. Maintaining family traditions, now that families no longer live settled lives on the land in one locality, does not have the same significance. And producing more children, in an era when almost every child lives to maturity and the earth is already overcrowded, is no longer a vitally important goal. The ideals of democracy, on the other hand, have now led people to expect marriage to bring them a relationship of love, intimacy, and fulfillment. Such a relationship, however, is very difficult to achieve, because it requires an understanding of what sociologist Nelson Foote called "interpersonal competence." So marriage is, temporarily at least, in a state of serious crisis in our culture.

I can sympathize wholeheartedly with Christian people who, in our present cultural situation, feel that the only course to take is to go back to the past and reinstate the hierarchical marriage. I do not believe, however, that this can actually happen. It not only flies in the face of our belief in democracy and personal freedom, but also runs counter to the progress of the movement to give full personhood to women—a social change which I think can now never be reversed nor ever should be.

However, there is another point which, for Christians, is of even greater importance. I believe, as I have tried to point out in this chapter, that the message of Jesus fully supports the transition, in marriage and the family, from the authority-obedience system to the love-trust system. The one item that has been a problem is our seeming inability to manage constructively the interpersonal conflict in a two-vote marriage. But now that we are beginning to understand the complex role of anger in marriage and to develop the means to use it creatively as raw material for growth, the final barrier is, at least theoretically, removed; and today we are seeing enough highly enriched Christian marriages to know that at last we have the answers.

Of course, it will take a long time, at the present slow rate of progress, to put these new insights to work. But I begin to see the possibility that in this endeavor the Christian community, which is much more deeply committed to the support of marriage than its secular counterpart, may lead the way. With this exciting possibility in mind, it seems unfortunate that some Christian husbands and wives, in the sincere and earnest belief that they are furthering the Christian cause, should in fact be doing the reverse.

What we need today, and need urgently, is a widespread movement that will produce large numbers of Christian marriages that really provide working models of the teaching of Jesus about creative love in human relationships.

PART 2

Managing Anger

chapter 5

Anger Patterns and Processes

If anger in itself is not sinful, but offers raw material for growth and change, how do we go about using it for this purpose? Any two people angrily confronting each other as adversaries have, theoretically, four choices. In practice, however, this may not always be true, because by the time they get into a conflict, the way in which they will behave is almost certainly predetermined by the pattern of interaction they have already established between them. Also, only three of those choices are available to a married couple, because they have taken the step of involving themselves in a shared life. I will, however, refer briefly at the end of this chapter to the fourth choice—the process of *dissolving* anger by detaching yourself from the other person and deciding that the relationship is simply not worth being angry about!

Let us now return to John and Mary and rescue them from the distressing situation in which we left them.

Three Ways To Deal With Anger

1. *Venting Anger.* As we have seen, the condition of being angry is a state of readiness to commit an act of aggression. In

marriage this is likely to be motivated either by fear or by frustration, or by a mixture of both.

John may fear that Mary will use this occasion to make him change by giving up his easygoing, untidy pattern of behavior; or he may fear that her indignation will goad her into telling other people, particularly her parents, that he is a sloppy, irresponsible individual. However, it is much more likely that he is frustrated and irritated because this present situation is disturbing the normal easygoing pace of his life. He is probably annoyed because Mary has so far been reasonably tolerant of his pattern, but now she is suddenly taking a very critical view of it. Certainly he is blaming her parents as the cause of this disturbance, even if innocently so. He is wishing they would cancel their proposed visit, and he is tempted to punish Mary by being really mean to them if and when they do come. He is stubbornly determined not to let Mary use this situation to gain control over him, and he has resolved not to act submissively in response to the dominant role she has assumed. He is ready to fight her on that issue.

Mary, for her part, is anxious to prove to her parents that she has made a good marriage and chosen a good partner, but she is afraid that if John doesn't put on a better performance they may conclude that she hasn't done so well after all, or that she has been unable to improve John's behavior in an area where they know that she herself has high standards. She is frustrated because John isn't willing to change his behavior, at least while her parents are with them, and thus support her. She fears that his unwillingness to do this may reveal that he doesn't love her as devotedly as she hoped he would, and this makes her feel that maybe after all she isn't as great a prize to him as she had imagined. Mary is therefore feeling somewhat insecure, but doesn't want to show this in case John interprets it as weakness and despises her for it. She has doubts as to whether she is going to win him over, but she is determined not to give in easily. So she also is prepared to put up a fight, though not at all sure that she is going to win.

If they do have a fight, what is likely to happen? Mary may keep up the battle for a time but then cry with vexation, which is a good way of shutting off all further discussion and making the other person feel like a heel. John may fall for this and make a few concessions, unwillingly but in order to end an unpleasant experience. The issue will then be set aside, but is likely to recur at a later time. They will both be hurt, and not much will have been achieved.

2. *Suppressing Anger.* This is the policy of avoiding the issue—"Peace at any price," or "Just forget it." All difficult or painful situations are swept under the rug, and nothing ever gets openly and honestly settled.

If John follows this course, he may suggest to Mary that they should avoid getting into an unpleasant situation that will only make them both mad. He may suggest that they talk no more about it now, because doing so is only making them upset. He may say in a half-hearted way that he'll try to be a bit less untidy, and then do nothing about it, or make such small improvements that they are just about back where they were before. He may suggest that they forget about the whole thing and offer to take her out to dinner to cheer her up. In one way or another, he will probably act evasively.

If Mary takes this line, she may stop pressing John to change and seem to drop the whole question, but inside she will feel martyred and decide to take up her cross and bear her burden with fortitude. Though she really feels mad at John, she will swallow her indignation, give him the silent treatment, and become more obsessed than ever about tidiness in order to demonstrate that, although *he* won't cooperate, *she* intends nobly to keep the flag flying. She will probably have a splitting headache and ask John to bring her an aspirin.

3. *Processing Anger.* If they are fortunate enough to adopt this course, John and Mary will agree to sit down together, now or later, and look at the whole situation as objectively as possible. Each in turn will share with the other just what is going on in his or her inner thoughts and feelings. They will

ask for feedback from each other to make sure that their messages are getting through. They will avoid any accusations of each other, sharing only what they are personally feeling and what they would like to have happen. When they are sure that all their feelings are out in the open, they will try to list all possible options and then narrow down their choices to the one on which they can reach the highest level of agreement.

Consider some options: John might agree to be exemplary while the parents' visit lasts, in return for a fair exchange in the form of something which Mary is willing to do for his benefit. Mary could agree to examine her rigid attitude to tidiness, which might be unreasonably compulsive and could be a source of real trouble later when there are children scattering playthings in the home. Along the same line, they might agree on defining a "halfway house" policy, with John tightening up his standards somewhat and Mary relaxing hers. Whatever they decide, it would be an experimental solution to be watched and evaluated again from time to time.

What processing anger does is to say in effect—"We got angry with each other, and we need to find out exactly why. Anger is a secondary emotion, usually triggered off by one or more underlying primary emotions. Let's try to explore our anger to get back to the primary emotions—fear, frustration, lowered self-esteem, hurt feelings, etc.—that produced the anger in the first place. Then let's see how we can help each other work through those deeper feelings. And let's follow through on this from time to time and check to see if we're making headway."

In other words, anger will never be sinful if we learn to make it the servant of our love and use it creatively to promote the growth and enrichment of our relationship.

Two analogies may be helpful:

1. Anger is like the smoke-alarm signal in your house. It warns you when there is danger and enables you to take appropriate action.

2. Anger is like the squeak in the motor of your car, which

tells you that something needs to be fixed. Attend to it, and the car will run better than ever. Ignore or avoid it, and you may end up with a breakdown on a lonely road on some dark and stormy night.

We may now assume that John and Mary have, in one of the three ways open to them, dealt with the crisis with which they were confronted. But we must not conclude that the issue that caused the crisis has therefore been settled. Moreover, this is only one issue. There are plenty of other areas in their relationship which are capable of creating new anger situations. So unless they understand the process of working through and adjusting their differences, and unless they use wisely the skills they will need for identifying and dealing with the areas where close contact with each other is sure to produce aggressive impulses, they are going to be denied the opportunity to achieve the loving, warm, and intimate relationship which both of them, in their hearts, earnestly desire.

In that critical process of growing together, anger should be their most reliable guide. It will identify accurately for them each new area of adjustment on which they need to work, and this will enable them to carry out together the growth process that will make their relationship more and more rewarding as the years go by.

But if they believe that anger is an enemy, and not a friend, how will they fare? If they choose to deal with their anger either by venting or suppressing it, what chance will they have of processing their feelings, identifying their unmet needs, and together developing a cooperative approach to their growth as individuals and as a couple?

The answer, alas, is that if John and Mary lack these insights and the skills they make possible, their chances of achieving a really good relationship, in which they develop their full potential for love and intimacy, will be poor indeed. In this they will not be at all exceptional. Perhaps 90 percent of all married couples are living well below the level of their relational potential. If present rates continue, about 40 percent of all couples presently married (in the U.S.) will ultimately divorce. If we assume that 10 percent will achieve their full potential, with or without help or guidance, that leaves 50 percent unaccounted for. A good many of these, although they will not break up, will achieve mediocre relationships, and some of their marriages will be deplorably poor. We need to remember that the alarming figures about battered wives refer to marriages that are still intact—it isn't easy to go on battering a wife from whom you are already separated!

Obviously the root cause of family violence lies in accumulated anger which piles up to explosive proportions. Once we understand how much anger the marriage relationship generates, and how little guidance and help couples receive about dealing with it constructively, family violence is not at all surprising. The tragic fact is that most of it could be prevented by training couples to understand and use the resources I am trying to make available in this book.

Difference, Disagreement, Conflict—A Recapitulation

Because of its vital importance, let us review, in more detail, what John and Mary need to know and to act upon.

First, they need to accept the fact that *there are differences between them which are capable of bringing about a clash of wills.* There is nothing wrong or unfortunate about that. It occurs in *all* marriages—even when husband and wife come from very similar backgrounds. No two people are entirely alike; and if such people existed and married each other, the marriage might turn out to be rather dull.

It would make sense for any couple, as they move into marriage, to identify the differences between them that are sure to cause them trouble, to make a list of them, and to take time to explore thoroughly their potential for troublemaking. For example, I am a person who likes to live at a pretty fast tempo—moving ahead and getting things done; while Vera is a much more contemplative person who just cannot be hurried. This difference has given us endless trouble, but we have worked on it steadily through the years. I have learned to be much more relaxed, while Vera is now an unusually punctual person in managing time and keeping appointments.

Second, John and Mary need to understand how, *under certain conditions, differences will become disagreements.* When they want to do things *together*, to get close and share their lives more deeply, they must reduce their living space and become more confined. It is exasperating that becoming more intimate should increase and intensify our areas of disagreement, but it is a fact of life that has to be faced. Intimacy is not a free gift—it has a price.

Third, John and Mary should recognize that disagreements are really hard to settle in ways which respect the freedom and personhood of both parties. *As a disagreement is confronted, it can very easily heat up and become a conflict.* The heat, of course, is generated by anger—all the bodily changes we have already described. Once anger has taken over, the relationship is really in danger, and no effective solution can be reached until the aggressive impulses have abated. To aid in this cooling-down process, it may be advisable to give each other more space temporarily and return later to address the issue. As a marriage counselor I have often advised that as soon as one member of a couple is aware of unmanageable emotional tension, he or she should raise the right hand as a silent signal to disengage; both should then, without any spoken word, go to different rooms and not resume communication until the angry partner is calm again. Of course that is not a resolution of the conflict—it simply takes the heat out and avoids exchanges that would be damaging and unprofitable.

An issue can seldom be helpfully handled while it remains hot. The first rule in dealing with a conflict is to take the anger out. In a state of hot anger it is impossible to be loving, caring, and understanding because you don't really hear your partner, you only see your own point of view, and you want your own way. Hot anger and objective thinking just don't go together.

Anger-Suppression as a Life Style

Disengaging to prevent the venting of anger, though it avoids needless pain, solves nothing; the disagreement is still there, as large as life. Failure to understand this leads many people into a trap. Shrinking from the heat and pain of vented anger, they resort to the suppressing of anger as a solution, and this then becomes an established habit.

Timid people, as well as many religious husbands and wives, adopt anger-suppression as a life style. Keeping aggressive urges under firm control is entirely possible. Indeed, there are many situations in which it is obviously the sensible thing to do. If your boss reprimands you, you are wise to reflect upon the undesirable consequences that might follow if you yelled back at him or punched his nose. This power to control anger is necessary and desirable, and we all have it—except for a few rare exceptions. Medical research has found that for a very few specially handicapped people, control of anger is impossible because a neuron circuit in the brain, or the endocrine system, is out of control.

Don't, however, be too ready to believe those people who say they have an "uncontrollable temper." The truth usually is not that they *can't* control their anger, but that they *won't*. Some people find early in life that throwing a temper tantrum is a highly effective device for getting their own way or for attracting attention. Children often discover this and use it. But if nothing is gained by this behavior, the device is soon abandoned.

Suppressing anger can become a habit—and it is a bad habit. In fact, it can be quite harmful. I have been a professor in two medical schools and have dealt with quite an interesting selection of people suffering from psychosomatic illnesses caused entirely by the persistent suppression of anger. In some cases, the recognition of what was happening was so effective that an apparently miraculous cure of the psychosomatic symptoms surprised and delighted my medical colleagues. We now know, of course, that a substantial number of illnesses are caused partially or entirely by emotional stress, and the habitual suppression of anger is a very common cause of such stress.

However, in marriage the habitual suppression of anger, often found in timid obedient wives but also in some husbands, can cause another kind of trouble. In my long years of marriage counseling I have observed that husbands and wives who habitually suppress anger lose, over the years, their capacity for emotional warmth and tenderness. In those marriages there are no fights, no arguments, and in the end no overt disagreements. Some of these people, and their relatives and friends, believe that these are happy marriages because the couples "never have a cross word." This is far from the truth. The marriages are sterile—totally without warmth or sparkle. It seems that a persistent state of low-key hostility and resentment has utterly destroyed spontaneous love. Yet the couples, having no alternative, continue to put up a front which suggests that they are happily and harmoniously united.

Helping these people is quite difficult, because they appear to have no troubles. They have staged a mutual withdrawal from emotional functioning at the interactional level; and apart from an illness or other overt manifestation of need, they have little motivation to seek help. A couple engaged in violent fights are obviously in trouble. Yet although their situation appears to be much more serious, I doubt that it is. Even those who "batter" each other are not necessarily as alienated as those who have simply closed each other out emotionally. I believe that people who have "frozen up" inside can only get back in touch with their feelings by being able to vent their anger as a stage in their recovery.

I recall the wife of a couple with whom I was counseling: she arrived for her interview one evening in a condition so lively that I was at first taken aback. Exultantly she reported that, as a result of being "freed up" during the previous interview, she had "shaken herself loose" and then, in the empty house, had gone around for an hour slamming doors and pouring out a torrent of abusive words. This had enabled her to feel and experience her anger for the first time since she was a child. Needless to say, she didn't need to continue this performance. She was soon in real touch with her aggressive feelings and able to share them in a more moderate manner with her husband.

What About "Marital Fighting"?

For married couples, I believe that neither venting anger nor suppressing it are helpful procedures, although the former, within reasonable limits, is healthier than the latter. However, George Bach has for many years advocated "marital fighting," and in his best-known book, *The Intimate Enemy*, has described elaborate techniques which couples can either try out for themselves or learn by attending his California clinic. Bach is a well-qualified psychologist and marriage counselor, and his books reveal that he has studied the subject of anger carefully and extensively. He is often quoted as an authority in the field.

My complaint about George Bach is mainly confined to the title of his training course and of his book. The idea of learning to "fight fair" in marriage is intriguing, and the idea of your spouse as your "enemy" is startling. In fact, however, Bach does *not* believe in marital fighting. By the time you have learned all the techniques and followed all the directions, you are not fighting at all, in the commonly understood sense of the term. For example, no one must on any account "win" in a marital fight! Can you imagine boxers or wrestlers being put in the ring and told to dance and roll about with each other, but warned not to hurt each other and on no account to win the fight?

What concerns me is that people hear that a distinguished marriage counselor advocates couples fighting each other, and as a result feel that this gives them permission to attack their spouses with full justification. And the title "The Intimate

Enemy" is a ridiculous example of contradictory terminology. No one can, as I understand the term, be "intimate" with an enemy; and no one would want to be at enmity with a person with whom an intimate relationship has been established. The book is a long one, nearly four hundred pages, and my fear is that many people will not read enough of it to discover that the cover is not at all descriptive of the contents.

A more serious complaint about Bach's "marital fighting" is that made by Murray Straus, whose pioneering work opened up the study of family violence. He quotes Jane Howard's description of a training session led by Bach, who said to one wife: "Don't be afraid to be a real shrew, a real bitch! Get rid of your pent-up hostilities! Tell them where you're really at! Let it be total, vicious, exaggerated, hyperbole!"[1] Murray Straus is concerned, because his own research has established clearly the fact that couples who vent their anger on each other tend, over time, to step up the vigor of their vocal attacks to the point where they cease to be effective, and they then spill over into the use of physical violence. So encouragement of the process of "getting rid of your pent-up hostilities" could actually be moving you in the direction of "battering" your spouse.[2]

In any case, I agree with the further comment of Straus that the idea that you "get rid of" your anger by venting it is open to question. As I observed earlier, the "ventilation" concept of "getting your anger out" is really a message to your body to keep it coming.

The "marital fighting" concept has, unfortunately, been widely promoted and widely accepted. Again and again I have seen it written about in women's magazines, and even commended by responsible professional writers. Israel Charney for example, writes, "The critical point of the hour, we have felt, is the need for a theory of marriage that acknowledges once and for all that marital fighting is inevitable, necessary, and desirable."[3]

The tragedy is that most people are aware of only two alternatives in the management of anger—venting or suppressing. Both, in my judgment, are undesirable and ineffective, but for most couples they appear to be the only options. This sorry state of affairs is likely to continue unless they can begin to see the processing of anger as valuable raw material to aid the growth of an intimate relationship. I suppose Vera and I would still be where they are if we had not happened to explore the subject diligently; and because we were profoundly dissatisfied with the two available alternatives, we discovered this far better way. We have kept hoping that we would find others who had made the same discoveries we have, and we *have* encountered a few who shared with us some of our new concepts. But we have still failed to encounter any statement that fully covers the field, a dilemma which finally led me to the decision to write this book.

Couples With Mixed Approaches

We have seen that different people handle anger in close relationships in different ways. The ventors let all their aggressive feelings out, often with a bang. The suppressors bottle up their feelings until they go sour and poison them inside. And the processors try to use their anger as raw material for relational growth.

A very practical question now arises: How do different combinations of these approaches affect a marriage?

When two ventors marry, obviously they are going to have a lot of fights. With reasonable control, these may not be as unpleasant as they sound. As a marriage counselor, I have often said that I could feel more hopeful about a couple who were throwing the furniture at each other than about a couple who were coldly ignoring each other. The furniture throwers are at least interacting, and this gives us something to work with! And for such couples, the making-up process after the fight is sometimes very warm and loving. At best, however, such marriages enjoy no more than a series of agreeable experiences, punctuated with periodic explosions. We sometimes call this the "yo-yo marriage"—a process of alternating closeness and distance, with constant movement and change. I even recall one psychologist who declared that fights are necessary for married couples, because they need to get away from each other from time to time in order to achieve distance. It seems not to have occurred to him that couples who communicate effectively can, and do, negotiate their distancing needs without requiring a fight to get them separated!

When two suppressors marry, they adopt the peace-at-any-price, everything-under-the-rug policy. These couples are soon frozen into emotional distance, and nothing but a major crisis can make anything significant happen between them. They are usually solid, law-abiding citizens, and include a fairly high proportion of church members.

When two processors marry, they have an ideal combination. Their relationship is dynamic, with everything out in the open, all anger situations faced and resolved, and all crises worked through together. If you know such a couple well, you can literally watch them grow. I have had the privilege of being in close touch with a number of such couples over the years, and it is a joy to know them and to see them progressively keeping their relationship up to full potential. (A couple's marital potential is not a fixed point, because it moves upward as *they* move upward!) I have also been able to watch couples who have just discovered together how to process their anger and have seen them move, sometimes from a very low point, into a phase of steady and continuing growth.

What about a ventor and a suppressor married to each other? This match, unfortunately is not unusual. It is the tyrant-slave relationship. The ventor finds he is unopposed and uses his power to keep his partner meekly and even abjectly obedient. You will notice that I said "he"—that is the usual pattern. However, there are occasional couples in which the wife is the ventor and the husband the suppressor. Such a wife is sometimes called a shrew, as demonstrated in Shakespeare's play on this theme. Another fictional character, developed in a newspaper cartoon, is Caspar Milquetoast, representing the husband in this kind of marriage.

We must remember, of course, that this type of union, with the husband the ventor, is the prototype of the traditional hierarchical marriage. All the major cultures, and their religions, have imposed this pattern on couples by law and custom. This pattern served a good purpose—the maintenance of stability in families—but the price that had to be paid was the denial of full personhood to women, who were portrayed as soft, timid, yielding creatures. I have never encountered any evidence that, under equal provocation, a woman generates less anger than a man does. But powerful social conditioning strove to turn all women into suppressors, and came very near to succeeding.

What About Dissolving Anger?

I have already indicated that there is a fourth way of dealing with anger. I call it *dissolving*.

Dissolving is a useful process in clearing up anger which is directed against persons or groups of persons with whom you are not closely related in terms of intimacy or love. The process is to detach yourself from the situation and accept no concern about it nor involvement in it. When that can be done, the aggressive feelings simply dissolve away, without any ill effects. However, this is never desirable, and seldom happens, in a close relationship, so it is not a primary issue for this book.

Yet while the dissolving of anger has very limited use between married couples, there is one type of situation in which it can play an important role. This is where, for some good reason, the processing of an anger situation must be unavoidably postponed. For example, Vera and I have found that one of us may become angry with the other at a time when we can do nothing about it. Immediate demands of our schedule or the presence of other people make it impossible to communicate directly the fact that one of us is angry. Provided there is no evasion of the fact that the issue *will* be shared as soon as an opportunity arises, temporary detachment from the anger situation can serve to dissolve the strong emotion for the time being; this is something quite different from suppression.

Even on occasions when it would be possible to find time to process anger, we have sometimes found that we cannot do so there and then because our feelings are "too hot to handle." This can be communicated to the partner, and an agreement reached to hold the processing till later. Such an agreement may even extend to setting aside the scriptural injunction "not to let the sun go down" on unprocessed anger. There are some situations that can be much better dealt with the next day, when we are both refreshed after a night's sleep and when we can see the issue in clearer perspective. In fact, experienced couples with a good relationship can be somewhat flexible about the rules as long as they are sure they are not suppressing anger, which is always an unhealthy process because it produces alienation and leaves the issue unresolved.

I have occasionally encountered couples who developed a secondary conflict about this approach. The husband, let us say, acknowledges that he is angry, but he needs time to clarify his thoughts about his feelings and wants the processing to be postponed. For the wife, however, this is unacceptable. She wants the issue faced and cleared up there and then. If her wish is denied, she then gets angry because he is angry and won't immediately get together with her and clear it up! This certainly complicates their task by giving them a double anger situation to process. But the principles I have enunciated still provide the answer.

Although normally the dissolving of anger is not applicable to the marital relationship today, I believe it has played an important part in earlier times. For example, I am sure that some of those traditional wives managed to cope with their tyrannical husbands, and to keep themselves emotionally sweet and wholesome, by this means. They remained emotionally detached from their husbands, but met their own needs for love and intimacy as mothers and as good neighbors and in their religious faith.

One very unusual case demonstrates a married couple using this approach. The husband, a devout Catholic, told me that whenever he and his wife became angry with each other, they withdrew separately by agreement for a period of prayer, during which they confessed to God their sinfulness in being angry with their spouse and asked for divine forgiveness. They then returned and resumed the marriage relationship, with no report or discussion of the issue. In this way, they claimed to have a convenient means of dealing with anger.

As I pointed out to the husband, however, this approach is based on the belief that anger is always sinful. And it offers no possibility of using the anger to deepen and improve the relationship. There is no direct sharing or reconciliation between husband and wife, no opportunity for each to become aware of the inner life of the other, and therefore no chance for dynamic growth in the marriage. I found out, on inquiry, that the couple had been taught this procedure by a group of Catholic sisters dedicated to the celibate life. Without doubt they offered the best they had, but alas, it was not the right approach for a married couple.

chapter 6

A Program for Relational Growth

Coping creatively with anger in marriage is part of a broader task—the overall improvement of the marriage relationship, which includes better communication, better cooperation and teamwork, increased mutual appreciation and affection, better sex, and more open sharing of feelings.

The discoveries which Vera and I made about anger would probably never have happened if we had not been working to enrich our relationship at *all* levels. Processing anger is only a part of the total task, although I am now convinced that it is the most important part.

The Marriage Enrichment Movement

In the 1960s Vera and I became interested in what is now called the marriage enrichment movement. We were at the time Executive Directors of the American Association of Marriage Counselors (now the American Association for Marriage and Family Therapy), a position which we held for seven years. The development of marriage counseling had up to that time been the primary focus of our professional interests. But as such counseling became widely accepted, and high training standards made it possible to produce well-qualified counselors to help married couples in serious trouble, we began to think in terms of the next stage—matching our skilled remedial services with corresponding preventive services.

Accordingly, we led our first weekend enrichment retreat for couples in 1962, and have since then worked with many small groups of couples who were not in serious trouble, but were interested in making their relatively satisfying marriages better still. These experiences made us realize how far short of their relational potential most marriages are and how much can be done to give them new insights, new resources, and new skills.

As we continued these programs, we began to better understand not only the possibilities for growth that exist in every marriage, but also how this concept has been given little attention because our culture has viewed the marriage relationship only in *static* terms. The prevailing concept is that you get married and "settle down"! It soon became clear to us that marriage is indeed a very *dynamic* relationship, constantly needing to adapt to individual changes in the partners, to changes in the cultural environment, and to the successive stages in the life cycle. We saw that few marriages stand still. Most are either getting better or getting worse.

We also began to understand why so many marriages fail —because the couple embark upon a complex and difficult task, with a terribly inadequate comprehension of what the task is and how to go about it. We found couples who were indeed working hard to make their marriages succeed, but were failing hopelessly because the thrust of their efforts was in a direction where nothing was likely to be achieved. We saw that most couples today are embarking upon marriage with little more equipment than couples had a century ago, although the task is now much more complex and the behavioral sciences have in the meantime provided us with a whole new set of resources to aid us. Yet our thinking about marriage is still shrouded in myths that bear little relationship to reality and taboos that discourage inquiry and investigation.

Ten Myths About Marriage

To illustrate the widespread confusion in our thinking, here are ten commonly accepted misconceptions about marriage:

1. *Marriages are made in heaven.* This is the romantic illusion that just because two people are attracted to each other and go through a wedding ceremony, some special dispensation spares them the toil and effort that are normally necessary for success in most other human undertakings. All couples awaken from this rosy but deceptive dream sooner or later—usually by the end of the first six months.

2. *A wedding is a marriage.* We often use the words *wedding* and *marriage* interchangeably, talking about "getting married" when we should say "getting wedded." A wedding is only the *beginning* of the task of achieving a marriage. In the U.S. today, about two-and-a-half million men and women annually report to a court of law that they have had a wedding but have failed to achieve a marriage, and they now want their agreement cancelled.

3. *Married couples must accept what happens to them "for better or for worse."* These words imply that some impersonal fate decides the issue for them. Not at all. Whether their marriage turns out to be better or worse than the average is decided by what the couple themselves make of the resources they bring to each other.

4. *Couples must be "compatible" for a marriage to succeed.* There is some truth in this. But the idea, first started by Plato, that the "right" couples fit each other like pieces of a jigsaw puzzle, is nonsense. Every marriage must involve a long process of mutual adaptation which may take most of a lifetime.

5. *Don't expect behavior changes in your marriage partner.* It is true that putting pressure on your spouse to change will be ineffective. But couples who *work together* can achieve remark-

able changes. It is now known that even very old people can change their behavior if they are effectively motivated and suitably rewarded.

6. *Happily married couples never disagree.* All couples have disagreements. Happy couples are those who have developed the skills necessary to resolve their differences amicably, while couples who avoid and suppress disagreements are not happy.

7. *Couples who stay together must be happily married.* The view that "stable" marriages are necessarily successful is now unacceptable. Many couples who don't divorce might have more and better reasons for doing so than many who do split up.

8. *Don't unload your personal problems on your spouse—keep them to yourself.* If marriage partners can't seek sympathy and support from each other in the ups and downs of life, who can they turn to? A loving, caring relationship involves everything that concerns the couple.

9. *Married couples should never discuss their marital difficulties with other couples.* We call this the "intermarital taboo," and it deprives couples of all kinds of mutual support and help which they could otherwise be giving each other.

10. *You don't need marriage counseling until you are in really serious trouble.* By that time it may be too late, because alienation has undermined the couple's motivation to work at the relationship. The counselor can do most for those who seek help early.

Finding Some Answers

The concept of growth in relationships appeals to many couples. In their heart of hearts, these couples know that their relationship has not turned out as they had hoped, and the idea that it could still do so reawakens for them a dream they had given up. However, when they realize that their goals in marriage, as in anything else, can be attained only by learning a set of new concepts and then working hard to put them into practice, discouragement often returns. Yet some are ready to make the commitment to ongoing growth when they see clearly the areas they must work on and the precise nature of the task. These areas, of course, differ from one marriage to the next, and each couple must find out for themselves just what their agenda is. Over and over again, we have found that they cannot do this until effective communication has been opened up between them. So, after they have made a commitment to growth, the couple should get training in couple communication (see Appendix).

Although effective communication is a major milestone on the road to better marriage, it is not the final destination. We used to think that if a couple could communicate effectively, they were ready to get on with the job of enriching their marriage. Now we know that this is not necessarily so. Many couples, faced with the need to communicate in greater depth, find themselves blocked. Why? Because when they begin to open up to each other, they reactivate old, unresolved conflicts, and this becomes very painful to them. As they try to grapple with these issues, they find themselves in disagreement, and then anger develops and heats it all up. At that point they are in danger of giving up and sinking back into lethargy. The field of marriage in our culture is, regrettably, littered with shattered dreams and abandoned hopes. The roadblock that is preventing millions of couples from realizing their legitimate expectations for a happy and successful marriage is their inability to process their anger in any effective manner.

A Plan for Your Marriage

In this chapter, therefore, I want to suggest a specific course of action that Mary and John might follow in order to develop a really successful marriage. I will talk to them directly, and to any other couple willing to listen.

A good way to begin would be to find out about the marriage enrichment movement. There are books to read, and some are listed and described in the bibliography. But books can only give you *ideas*; it is *action* that will really bring growth. So after some basic reading and discussions, it would

be very helpful to participate together in a marriage enrichment event. Quite a number of national organizations are now
offering programs in this field, and some of them are listed at
the end of this book (see Appendix). The value of an experience of this kind is that it puts you in touch with other couples
who are also working together on their marital growth; it also
gives you an *experiential*, rather than an informational, intro-
duction to the field of marriage enrichment.

Beware, however, of those who suggest that the marriage
enrichment weekend will perform some miracle that will
change your life. It won't. Nobody's life ever changed in a
weekend. You may get the mountaintop vision of the way you
want to go, but you have to follow through by taking the long
road, a step at a time.

To make it as clear as possible, let me suggest that you give
yourselves at least a year to get well started on a new course.
By the end of that time, if you have really taken it seriously,
you should see enough difference in your relationship to prove
to you that it works. Accept this as a challenge if you like. You
have nothing to lose.

The program I offer you is what Vera and I have already
carried out and are continuing to follow. It involves more than
just processing anger; but we have found that the processing of
anger is the key that really turns the lock and opens the door.

In the year ahead, I would suggest that you make your
utmost effort to do three things; pledge to each other now that
you will do them faithfully together:

1. *Get together every day for a "sharing time."* I can hear you
say, "How can we ever, with the pressures now upon us,
squeeze out more time for something like this?" My answer is
that Vera and I, often with very heavy schedules, can't afford
not to have our sharing period. The time it *saves*, by not later
having to clear up misunderstandings and get back in touch
with each other, alone makes it worthwhile, quite apart from
the positive gains it brings.

Actually, it needn't be a lot of time. Indeed, it shouldn't be.

It is *not* a time for general conversation, catching up with each other's news. It is *not* a time to report to each other on projects. It is *not* a time to work together on issues in your relationship. It is *not* a time to exchange ideas you may want to discuss.

What then is it? *It is a time to tell each other just what you are feeling right now.* No more, and no less, than that.

What good will that do? Try it and see. You'll be surprised. Most married couples just don't report their feelings to each other. They report where they went, what they did, who they met, how they interpret the latest news, what needs to be done, and so on. But their hopes and fears, their excitement and anxiety, their joy and sorrow, their pride and embarrassment, their apprehension, their feelings of inadequacy, and their *anger*—these, in most marriages, are seldom really shared, and then only casually. But these are the really important things about us, and certainly these are the things that need to be known and understood and shared by people who love each other.

Let me be quite specific. Twenty minutes in a day will be enough if you get right on with it. Each should take a turn—about ten minutes will do. Just relax and listen to the voices coming up from your inner self, the voices that are telling you where you are right now, which is what you and your partner need to know. Without self-awareness, you are not in charge of your own life—it's as simple as that. And without other-awareness you don't know where your partner is, and in consequence you don't know when to comfort, when to support, when to praise, when to help—the very things loving people do for each other.

Try this experiment. Each of you, separately, take a sheet of paper. In ten minutes write down every feeling you can identify—positive or negative, strong or weak, physical, emotional, aesthetic, spiritual. If you're in touch with your inner self, you should in that time identify eight or ten feelings. Put them all down. If there is one you *can't* write down, ask yourself why. (It's particularly important to share "pinches" you have had in the last twenty-four hours. I'll explain this in detail later. It's the way to catch anger situations before they can get out of hand.)

Now get together and share all the feelings you have recorded. Don't discuss them or analyze them. *Just report them.* Then go over each other's list and find out how many of these feelings you would have known your partner had, if he or she had not shared them. Then you'll begin to see why you need a daily sharing time.

Just *when* you have your sharing time doesn't matter, but it should be an *uninterrupted* time. We have ours first thing in the morning. Some couples have it last thing at night, or any time in between. Make it *pleasant*—over a cup of coffee, relaxed. But keep on doing it until it becomes a habit. Vera and I are now agreed that we would soon be out of touch with each other if we didn't do this *every day*. After a year, my guess is that you'll feel the same way about it.

2. *Make time to work through every issue that brings any kind of tension into your relationship.* This should *never be done in your sharing time*, though issues do come up then. Schedule a specific time for a major decision, a serious misunderstanding, an anger situation. It's a matter of keeping your relationship clear of clogging, disturbing, confusing, painful situations. The golden rule is: "nothing on the back burner."

I am referring, of course, to issues in your relationship that could alienate you if they are not cleared up. Face the fact that *you just can't afford to be alienated*. It costs too much in time, effort, hurt feelings, foolish actions, bad decisions, and misunderstandings.

Clearing up an issue is top priority. It justifies skipping a meal, losing some sleep, revising your schedule, canceling an engagement. The warmth and closeness of your love relationship is the powerhouse in both your lives, and if the power gets cut off, everything else is soon out of action. If you need to be really alone together, the cost of a night in a motel is a very worthwhile investment. If you find you can't cope alone together, bring in another trusted couple, or see a marriage counselor. But *don't drift apart and get alienated*. That can be the beginning of the end.

3. *Join a growth group with other couples, or start one of your own.* One of the most exciting discoveries I've made in recent years is that couples are really good for each other. I'm not referring to those dull, formal social get-togethers where everything is elegant and lavish and the conversation is utterly trivial. I mean a group of couples who are committed to sharing their experiences of marriage in order to help and support each other in growing closer together and enriching their relationships.

I have already referred to a myth which I call the "inter-marital taboo." It says, "When married couples get together, they must never, never, never tell each other what's going on in their relationships." It goes back to the time when people lived in small villages and had to safeguard their privacy. Today, it's a tragic barrier which prevents couples from sharing with other couples the most important things in their lives. We can testify that when couples relax the taboo and share honestly where they are, it can bring a marvelous sense of closeness and mutual support. So get into a couples' group if you can. We call it a support group, and the couples normally meet regularly (usually once a month) in each other's homes.

Don't fall into the trap of making it a "discussion group" or a "study group" based on a book (even this book!). That's all head stuff and won't get you very far. When a real support group meets, we each report just where we are in our relationships right now, and we share our joys and sorrows, our hopes and fears, our growing edges. Soon couples are identifying with each other, learning from each other, helping each other, caring deeply about each other.

Well, that's the program for a year. And when the year is over, plan for the next year. If you've used the time right, my guess is that it will be more of the same.

Act on the Pinch!

In conclusion, let me satisfy your curiosity about something I said earlier—about "acting on the pinch." Psychologists have now realized the importance of catching anger as early as possible, before it piles up. How does it start, and can we stop it there?

Consider John and Mary again. They are talking together. Suddenly John says something that gives Mary a twinge of pain. John may have done it intentionally, or he may not. Anyway, Mary feels hurt, put-down, demeaned.

What John did to Mary was a pinch. If he had pinched her physically, she would have recoiled and moved away out of reach. In just the same way, she now shrinks back, though not visibly. A tiny wave of resentment, annoyance, indignation pulses through her. This is a pinch—the first faint stirring of anger and alienation.

What should Mary do? She may say to herself, "After all, it's a very small twinge, and really not important. Is it worth mentioning?" She decides that it isn't. The conversation flows on, and the pinch is ignored.

Next day, Mary does something that annoys John. Again, it's only a mild annoyance, but it's a pinch. He says nothing since it hardly seems worth mentioning.

But evidence shows that pinches *are* worth mentioning. Each tiny experience of alienation is in itself of little importance. However, add them all up, day after day, week after week, and they can cause a couple gradually, almost imperceptibly, to drift apart. Their love cools.

Now suppose these pinches are acted on. Mary shares with John her reaction to what he said. He shares with her his disapproval of what she did. These responses must not be made harshly or critically, but gently, with an honest desire to understand. They talk it over quietly together. That may be enough. Or they delve deeper and discover something they hadn't previously been aware of. They decide to do something about it, and both feel comfortable and reassured. Instead of a small alienation, there is a small reconciliation. Both feel a new confidence because these small irritations can be openly shared, examined, and cleared up. Over time, dealing with pinches gradually brings them closer together. And there is no chance for small angers to accumulate and become big angers.

So learn to be free to say "I feel pinched." It may not be necessary, or convenient, to say it right away. Here is the value of the daily sharing time. Often it is easier to say, "I felt pinched yesterday, and I'd like to share it with you." Then describe what happened. No further discussion may be needed, unless it raises an issue to be investigated and cleared, and that should of course be done at another time. What is important, though, is that *all pinches have to be shared within twenty-four hours*, so there can be no buried resentment festering and poisoning the relationship, ending up with a major crisis.

We sometimes talk about an "intentional" marriage. We mean simply that the couple are working for the improvement of their relationship, with a specific, agreed plan and goals clearly stated for, say, a year ahead. They are not drifting, rudderless, like ships at sea with no clearly defined destination. As the years pass they check off goals that have been achieved, and then set new goals.

It's a good way to live. But you can't make it happen by wishing it would, or by dreaming about it, or even by talking about it together, though that's a good way to start. Even having the *intention* isn't enough in itself—the road to hell, somebody one said, is paved with good intentions!

There has to come a time when, being convinced, you *act* and act *together*. If in reading this book you have been convinced that you see new possibilities for your marriage relationship, you should understand very clearly that this will make little difference unless conviction is followed by appropriate action.

chapter 7

Coping With a Marriage Crisis

If John and Mary make a practice of acting on their pinches, draining away incipient anger before it can accumulate into an explosive mass of aggressiveness, they will greatly lessen their chances of having a major crisis in their relationship. But a crisis can still arise, despite every precaution they take. So in this chapter we will develop a plan for coping with such a situation. And our goal will be something more than simply getting the crisis over with so that they can go back to where they were before. The Chinese character for the word *crisis* is a combination of two separate characters—one meaning "danger," the other "opportunity." Our object will be to avoid the danger and to seize the opportunity—the opportunity to improve the relationship and to use the crisis as a growth point.

The first thing to understand is that a relational crisis can be effectively cleared up only by setting aside time to deal with it. Today's busy schedules often make this difficult to do. But there is no alternative. Far too many marriages degenerate from bad to worse just because *the couples concerned don't make time to clear up issues as they develop.* Just as we recognize the wisdom of making minor and major repairs to our homes as the need arises, so we should not neglect to make minor and major repairs to our marriages if we want them to go on working smoothly and bringing us the rewards we expect from them.

The sure signal that a repair may be needed is that one partner, or both, develops sustained anger toward the other. This is the great value of anger in marriage: it gives us accurate and clear notice that something needs to be adjusted and corrected.

The minor repairs are usually easy to deal with, especially if we make them as they arise. The major repairs require more time and effort. But a series of minor crises can easily pile up together and produce a major crisis. Or a major crisis, against the background of an accumulation of neglected minor crises, may present a couple with a formidable task.

Let us suppose that such a situation has arisen in your marriage, and both you and your spouse are upset and worried about it. You have recognized that it has to be dealt with, but the atmosphere is now tense, and you seem to be deadlocked. The whole issue has become so sensitive that you both begin to feel angry every time you think about it. How do you proceed?

First, choose a time and a place where you will definitely not be interrupted. Then begin by sharing your hurt feelings, without any reference to the issue that caused them—your distress, your pain, your anger. At this level you can identify with each other, even if so far you seem to have nothing else in common.

Now take the next step, which is to try to establish clearly what the issue really is. Keep strictly to the facts. When two people quarrel, they tend to support their case by dragging in other issues that don't really belong, or they expand the cause of annoyance by quoting past examples of similar situations. Thus John may say to Mary, "You're trying to make me over, and I won't stand for it. It isn't just the way I leave my clothes around; you put me down in other ways too. I've been noticing this lately. In fact, come to think of it, you've been acting that way ever since we got married. You always seize an opportunity to make me seem less capable than you are. You even did it sometimes before we were married. I think you got this habit from your mother. Have you noticed how she treats your dad?"

Under this catalog of complaints, Mary hasn't a chance. Stung by an injured feeling of injustice, her righteous wrath mounts, and she reaches in all directions for ammunition to fire back. A fight develops, and the original issue is lost in the barrage of other and irrelevant materials that get thrown in.

Some Practical Proposals

In order to avoid this kind of entirely useless and unproductive bickering, you need to protect yourselves by having some established principles. So, let's try to set down some ground rules:

1. *Cool down.* As long as either of you is in a state of hot anger, it will be almost impossible to make any progress. Only by taking the anger out of the conflict can you move back squarely to the disagreement and see it in perspective. So check up on each other: "Are you cool and calm now?" When you can both say "yes," you are ready to begin.

Here are some ways of cooling down. Relax in an easy chair or on a sofa—even lie on the floor. I remember reading about an experiment that was carried out with quarreling children. The researcher would locate two fighting kids out on the school playground. He would bring them inside and, in a pleasant room, have them lie down on comfortable cushions on the rug and relax. Then he would tell them that it was okay for them to go on with their quarrel. In each case, they laughed rather sheepishly and said they just weren't in the mood to go on fighting. Relaxed muscles encourage emotional calm. Find something you can laugh about together. Act lovingly, too—putting your arms around each other is a wonderfully effective antidote to aggressive impulses. Combine all three—then just try to be angry when you're in each other's arms on the floor and laughing together!

2. *Keep cool*. At this stage, agree that you won't attack, blame, or provoke each other, by word or deed. Communicate only with explanatory "I" messages, such as, "This is where I am right now." Don't use accusing "You" messages, like, "You are doing. . . ." "You have done. . . ." Agree that you're looking together for the basic difference between you that is creating the disagreement, and try to function for the time being as a neutral investigating committee preparing a report for the board of directors.

3. *Try to define the disagreement*. Put it in objective terms: "John would like to do it this way, but Mary would prefer to do it that way. They are both sincere about where they stand, and they are also eager to find a way of coping that can be acceptable to both of them, so that they can join in a united policy." This need not be done in precise detail—the real work has still to be undertaken.

4. *Prepare separate written statements in which you both put the other's point of view in words*. This may seem elaborate, but you will find in practice how effective it is. Each of you separately speaks for the other in statements that begin: "I, Mary. . . ," written by John; and "I, John. . . ," written by Mary. Usually it is best to separate and do this in different rooms, away from each other. Take all the time you need, and try to include all the vital concerns.

5. *Correct each other's statements*. Come together again and exchange what you have written. Each is then free to change or modify at any point the other's statement about where you are. Discuss and explain where necessary, but don't get into an argument about it. Each person *must* have the authority and right to finalize the statement that represents his or her position. Then give back the corrected statements and accept all corrections in good faith.

6. *List all available options.* Based on your now accurate knowledge of just where both of you are, each should now separately make a list of all possible courses of action that could be taken. There may be quite a number—we once had *nine* options! By the way, it may be best again to go to separate rooms for the listing of options.

7. *Come together again and choose the option on which you can reach maximum agreement.* Examine them one by one. Try to pick one that seems reasonably fair to both of you. The possibility must exist, however, that no available option will be acceptable to you both. If necessary, settle for an option that will be purely experimental and to which you will not be finally committed.

You may have a negative reaction to this suggested plan. The way to sabotage it is quite simple. All you have to do is to say, "This doesn't make sense to me. I'm sure it won't work, and I'm just not prepared to try it."

How do you know it won't work? All I ask is that you give it a fair trial. I have used this procedure with quite a number of couples, and they have often been amazed at how much they have been able to achieve. One couple came back, smiling broadly, and said, "It's all settled." Another couple, a little bewildered, reported that they had found that they didn't have a disagreement at all—they had just been confused by poor communication! I know that some people think the idea of writing things down is "gimmicky." Not so. It is a well-known fact that this is an excellent way of taking the emotional bias out of your thinking, making you more fair-minded, more likely to see straight.

Doing all this seems elaborate, I know. It can take a couple of hours, or even more. But some fights go on just as long as that, achieve nothing, and leave you both exhausted. So I repeat, give it a fair trial and find out for yourselves.

The Art of Negotiation

You will have guessed by now that there is a theoretical base behind all this. What I have given you is an exercise in *negotiation*. Negotiation is the key word, describing the only way in which disagreements can be resolved. This is true of all kinds of disagreements, at all levels—from a husband-wife conflict, to a management-labor dispute with a strike threatened, to a session in the United Nations to avert a world war.

When you negotiate, you are dealing with a disagreement. A difference, as we have seen, produces a disagreement when the parties seem unable to come close and reach a common mind, yet are too much involved just to walk away from each other. In other words, it is vital that they should reach agreement if their relationship is to continue in a cooperative manner.

You can't negotiate a conflict because angry people are emotionally stirred up and can't sit down together and be reasonable or objective. The anger must be taken out first, and then you are back with the disagreement.

When John and Mary are ready to negotiate, there is distance between them. They are in danger of being alienated, or they may already be alienated. They want to get back together, hand in hand. Negotiation offers them three possible choices:

1. *Capitulation.* This option requires one partner to move right over and stand alongside the other. One gives up nothing, the other gives up everything. This may sound very unfair. However, there are two quite distinct kinds of capitulation. One is a surrender brought about by the use of force— that's the bad kind. The other is a gift offered as an act of love—that's the good kind, and it can be especially effective in a marriage crisis.

Let's apply this to John and Mary. One of them could use power, or the threat of power, to coerce the other. John could say, "I absolutely refuse to change my behavior in order to make a favorable impression on your parents. When they come, I will just go on doing what I like." Mary then has no alternative but to swallow her indignation and nurse her hurt feelings. She suppresses her anger and puts on an act during her parent's visit. But she remains cold and distant toward John.

Or Mary might say, "I simply won't have my parents come here if you won't change. I'll cancel the visit and tell them why I'm doing so." Now John is in a box. He is going to be in the doghouse with his wife's parents and will have to face any punishment Mary inflicts on him—like no support, no affection, no sex. So he gives in, but *he* is angry, ready to get back at Mary in some way.

That's the bad kind of capitulation.

Now let's look at the good kind. John could say, "Okay, Mary, I see that this means a lot to you. I don't really want to change, but I love you and I want to make you happy. So I'll try to be tidy while your parents are here, though I won't promise to go on doing so afterwards." This represents a gift of love, freely and voluntarily given. It should make Mary very happy and grateful.

Or Mary could say, "I'm sorry I can't persuade you, John. But I don't want to make a major issue out of this. I love you too much to go on fighting with you, so I'll just give in gracefully." John will now feel good. He is getting his own way, and an affirmation of love from Mary into the bargain. He should be very appreciative.

Now a word of warning: Loving capitulation is a gracious gift between marriage partners. But over time, *it must be a two-way process*. If one does all the capitulating, the relationship may begin to assume a master-servant character. In most cases, however, the giving of gifts seems to be reciprocated, so the safeguard is there. I believe capitulation as a gift of love should always be the first option considered in any marriage crisis. It pleases both, and it disposes both to offer further gifts of love. It creates a good atmosphere in the marriage.

2. *Compromise*. If capitulation isn't possible, the next option is to try to find a middle position in which both surrender something and both gain something. This is the familiar process of bargaining, or horse-trading. We talk back and forth,

making concessions and gaining others, till finally we find a meeting point. I take less for my horse than I had hoped for, but I do find a buyer. You pay more than you intended, but you take the horse home with you.

A great deal of bargaining goes on in all marriages, whether or not it is recognized as such. It is probably the most common way of settling disagreements. It can even be fun.

For John and Mary, it might be settled by Mary letting John keep his study untidy, as he usually does, if he will not disarrange the more public areas of the house after Mary has put them in order for their visitors. Further, both agree that they won't start, or participate in, any discussion of their difference of opinion on this subject in the presence of Mary's parents. This means that each of them makes a concession to the other.

3. *Coexistence.* Situations can and do arise in which disagreements cannot be resolved by either capitulation or compromise. After full exploration, no way emerges in which either party can yield. *This state of affairs should be accepted only after each has made every possible honest and sincere effort to accommodate the other.* A deadlock in which neither is willing to budge an inch is a refusal to negotiate at all and can create very bad feelings. But if each is satisfied that the other has really tried to give ground wherever possible, but cannot do so without violating some important principle, a state of unresolved disagreement can often be accepted with a good grace.

Of course this may cause inconvenience and even distress to one or to both, but it may be better to live with this than to take the only other course available, which is coercion. We are, of course, speaking here of a *love relationship*; and it is one of my deep convictions that using power in such a relationship always damages love. And the repeated use of power ultimately destroys love. That is a price which I am not prepared to pay. To force a marriage partner to act against his or her best judgment, sincerely held, is to violate seriously his or her personhood.

So what? I can only say that Vera and I, over the years, have found that the passage of time brings new insights, and apparently deadlocked issues clear up as new perspectives develop. In some situations, too, it is possible to remove the disagreement by abandoning, by mutual consent, the project on which a united policy seems unattainable. This is similar to the process of dissolving anger by deciding that the issue is no longer relevant.

I am well aware that in many marriages these principles are considered to be of little or no importance. But that only helps to explain why so many couples in our culture have relationships of such poor quality. *Loving relationships take skill and patience* to achieve and to maintain; but the rewards they bring richly justify the efforts that are needed to achieve them.

chapter 8

Independence and Interdependence in Marriage

All human relationships are complex, and close relationships are particularly complex. I have sometimes said that marriage represents the equivalent of two universes interacting with each other. For those who are really committed to developing their full marital potential, the human life span is almost too short a time in which to learn all we need to learn about it.

Throughout our nearly twenty years of involvement in marriage enrichment, Vera and I have worked with well over a thousand married couples in small, intensive groups, at considerable depth, and over periods of as long as a week. We have kept records of most of the agenda items which they brought up for investigation, issues that represented their "growing edges." One that frequently occurs is what we have come to call "separateness and togetherness"—preserving a comfortable balance between the freedom of the individual partners to act independently and to develop their own individual patterns and abilities, while at the same time enjoying the rewards of a deeply shared life.

Marriage has been attacked vigorously in recent years as representing a form of bondage, particularly for the wife. There is no doubt that this accusation is fully justified in terms of the historical record. As we have seen, the stability of family life has been maintained in the major human cultures by making marriage a one-vote system; and in recent years, when the democratic ideal has insisted on changing it to a two-vote system, the effects of the change on the stability of the family have been devastating. I am aware that other cultural factors have contributed to family breakdown rates, but I have no doubt at all that this has been the main cause. And the insistence of the wife that she be given the status of a full partner does not represent the whole picture. Husbands also have been exasperated by the endless difficulties involved in trying to achieve a smoothly working partnership, and many of them have given up in despair, choosing instead, at least for a time, the relative simplicity of singlehood.

There can be no question that when the Declaration of Independence promised "life, liberty, and the pursuit of happiness" to every individual American, this represented the dawn of a new era in human history. The democratic ideal is not new, by any means, but its unqualified acceptance by what has become one of the leading nations of the world represents a milestone in human progress. Throughout history, we find innumerable instances of the suppression of individual freedom; and even today, the total number of nations granting liberty in any full sense to their citizens still represents a relatively small minority.

So there is no question in my mind that we are on the right track in fiercely defending human rights. As often happens, however, the pendulum seems now in danger of swinging too far, and our enthusiasm for individual fulfillment can cause us to forget the equally important principle of meeting our social obligations. Democracy, as I understand it, is a just balance between the achievement of basic individual rights and the discharge of basic social duties. If the modern doctrine of "neo-narcissism," as it has been called, should gain the ascendancy, we could find that we have simply exchanged the domination of a few major tyrants for that of a multitude of petty tyrants.

However, I don't expect this to happen, for the simple reason that our human needs are not best met by an overemphasis on independence, but by a comfortable balance between independence and interdependence—which brings us to the marriage relationship.

Love and Anger in Balance

In all our discussions with groups of couples, the conclusion has emerged clearly that a healthy marriage is one that provides both separateness and togetherness, both independence and interdependence. But an equally important conclusion is that while this is theoretically obvious, it proves in practice to be a difficult task.

My major thesis in this book is that *in every marriage the two dynamic forces are love*, which seeks to draw the couple together, *and anger*, which tends to drive them apart. I believe that both are present and active, from beginning to end. In the early period of marriage, they seem to be acting against each other. The strong pull of young love draws the couple closer and closer in quest of intimacy; and when anger develops as a counter force, it is perceived as something hostile and destructive—a sinister influence that blights the blossom of unfolding love.

Anger, however, being a healthy emotion, is really trying to play a helpful part. It is preserving the individual partner from a loss of personhood through the development of an unhealthy dependence on the mate. By pushing the couple apart, it insures the necessary distance to maintain their independence, while preserving the interdependence necessary for a meaningful relationship. If the role of anger in the marriage is rightly understood (which usually is not the case), the situation slowly changes, and anger becomes not the opponent of love, but its ally. It draws attention to those areas of the relationship where the two personalities do not "fit" each other, and where changes of behavior are necessary if love is not to be abraded by continual tension.

Here we reach the critical point in relational growth. If the couple do not understand the positive role of anger and simply respond to it by progressive distancing, they will slowly disengage and drift apart. This is precisely what is happening to millions of marriages in our culture today. It happens not, as some would have us suppose, because the people involved are somehow more wicked, or more irresponsible, than their parents were. It is simply that open disengagement from marriage is much easier today, and much less subject to social disapproval; and, in addition, the single life is being proclaimed in many quarters as the way to health and happiness (in spite of impressive evidence to the contrary). At the root of broken marriages, therefore, lies widespread failure to understand the positive role of anger in marriage.

For those who do understand the purpose of anger, a very different prospect opens up. As the marriage develops and the necessary interpersonal adjustments are made, the role of anger changes. It becomes the ally, and not the enemy, of love, continuing to guide the couple through the life cycle by calling for new adjustments in order to maintain and deepen their intimacy. Meanwhile, as love matures and becomes less and less possessive, it takes over some of the earlier roles of anger by freeing the couple from the danger of overdependence on each other. Couples in a state of immature love are often fiercely jealous and overprotective, whereas mature couples encourage individual freedom and development and take joy and pride in each other's separate achievements. Finally, love develops the strength to grant complete freedom, based on complete trust that it will not be abused or violated.

So independence and interdependence come into perfect balance, with love as a sustaining force, and the fine tuning of the relationship is still being promoted by the gentle prodding of anger.

The tragedy is that so many couples have no comprehension of this process. And they are so obsessed with the doctrine of independence, maintained by "assertiveness," that they cannot allow their love to attain any strength or depth. They keep insisting on the distancing process and reinforcing the anger that is already doing this for them. They taste love superficially, but reject it as soon as it seems in any way to threaten to bind them, on the false assumption that a sense of identity is best achieved through self-sufficiency.

The shallowness of this doctrine is revealed by the fact that separated and divorced persons tend again and again to turn back to remarriage or cohabitation in the quest for love. But often the combination of self-assertion and the distancing effect of anger block love's maturing and the only kind of intimacy they ever achieve is sexual intimacy, which, without interpersonal intimacy, has been described by Thomas Oden as being "like a diploma without an education."

Safeguarding Individual Freedom

In a mature marriage, therefore, anger loses its power to threaten or damage the relationship. For some couples the idea of treating anger as a friend, and not an enemy, sounds phoney. But I can testify that anger is really a friend.

Being angry is always an uncomfortable experience, and therefore unwelcome. But when its beneficent role is fully accepted, it is no longer feared. Indeed, the fear begins to diminish as soon as the couple make a contract never to attack each other when angry and when a sufficient period of time has elapsed to furnish convincing evidence that the contract holds. Once anger no longer threatens the relationship, the experience is like going through a sound barrier into a new sphere in which love is free to grow without hindrance.

This is not to say, however, that anger is left behind. As I have already said, anger will be with the couple to the end. As well as bringing to our notice the need to make new adjustments as life goes through inevitable changes, anger exercises its important distancing role, standing guard over our individual need for freedom and solitude.

There is a school of thought that sees a loving couple essentially in terms of unlimited closeness, and even talks of marriage as a *union of two personalities*. This concept may be permissible in poetry, but not in prose. On a realistic basis, the union of two persons would mean the annihilation of each; and no couple aspiring to love each other would be willing to pay that sort of price!

The separateness of the individuals in a marriage must be safeguarded. Fortunately, some poets have affirmed this. The much-quoted admonition of the Lebanese poet Kahlil Gibran, "Let there be spaces in your togetherness," makes the point succinctly. The German poet Rilke developed the same idea with more elaboration:

> It is a question in marriage, to my feeling, not of creating a quick community of spirit by tearing down and destroying all boundaries, but rather a good marriage is that in which each appoints the other guardian of his solitude, and shows him this confidence, the greatest in his power to bestow. But, once the realization is accepted that even between the closest human beings infinite distances continue to exist, a wonderful living side by side can grow up.

The Meaning of Intimacy

What, then, do we mean by intimacy? I have already mentioned the definition of "shared privacy," which, though brief, is surprisingly adequate.

A simple diagram called the Johari window is sometimes used by psychologists to portray the four different areas of the individual personality: what is known to the self alone, to the self and others, to others and not to the self, and neither to the self nor to others. A similar framework could be used to clarify the meaning of intimacy, confining the categories to the self and the marriage partner. Here is such a diagram: intimacy would mean having nearly everything in the top left corner.

WHAT IS KNOWN TO SELF AND TO MARRIAGE PARTNER	WHAT IS KNOWN TO SELF BUT NOT TO MARRIAGE PARTNER
WHAT IS KNOWN TO MARRIAGE PARTNER BUT NOT TO SELF	WHAT IS NOT KNOWN EITHER TO SELF OR TO MARRIAGE PARTNER

DIAGRAM BASED ON THE JOHARI WINDOW

When John and Mary first meet, their knowledge about each other is limited to what they can immediately observe, together with anything they have been told in advance. As they learn more through direct communication, they begin to identify more closely with each other, and the scope of their knowledge spreads rapidly. It is now known that deep friendships are based mainly on mutual self-disclosure. Therefore, as a couple's interest in each other increases, they reach a frontier—the defensive line enclosing what is considered their "private lives." Beyond this line exists all information that is not normally disclosed to others.

Some couples marry with these frontier lines intact, and even spend a lifetime together without taking down their defenses. Such relationships may be entirely satisfactory to the couples concerned, because their expectations of marriage may not include intimacy beyond this point. For such couples, there are two kinds of information not mutually disclosed: what they do not know about themselves, and what they choose to keep secret.

Secrets fall into two main categories. First, there is information about other people which has been confidentially disclosed; sharing this, even with a loved marriage partner, would be a breach of confidence. The other category consists of information about the self that is deliberately withheld.

We must focus upon this latter information in defining intimacy. The main reason for withholding private information about the self is a fear that if you told all, you might be downgraded in the eyes of your partner, whose love for you might diminish as a result. For an insecure person, this can be a terrifying possibility. Disapproval is, as we have seen, closely associated with anger; and it is indeed understandable that some married couples cannot bring themselves to take this risk. Yet if they cannot do so, the door to full intimacy remains closed. The ultimate validation of a person's identity comes only through a continuing relationship in which he or she is fully known and deeply loved. As long as husband and wife cannot make themselves totally vulnerable to each other, they cannot be totally relaxed, because somewhere a secret sentry stands before a closed door. And the door is closed because of a lurking fear of disapproval or rejection. Also, a lingering anxiety exists: "Will my mate somehow find out? Could I talk in my sleep and reveal my secret? Would I still be loved if my partner knew all?"

The final achievement of intimacy, therefore, comes when husband and wife can make themselves totally vulnerable, with no need to maintain a guard against the possibility of an angry attack or a disapproving rejection. All marriages do not achieve this degree of intimacy, by any means. But some do. And the experience of total trust that develops out of total intimacy, and assures both partners of total love, is marriage at its very best.

We have come a long way from the facile promises of the fairy tales, which seemed to make married love so easy and effortless, and from the slick promise of "instant intimacy" of a more recent era. Yet even in the fairy tale in which the gallant prince rescues the fair lady from the jaws of the dragon, we read that they then sat down together and "he told her all his heart."

The tendency today is to ridicule the romantic dreams about marriage that have appeared and reappeared in the legends and folk songs of all human cultures—stretching back to Chinese poetry in the fifth century B.C. I suggest that these dreams are not as unattainable as the cynics would have us believe. Rather, like every other worthwhile prize in life, there is a price to pay, in effort and in sacrifice, for their attainment. And, like the rich young ruler in the New Testament story, many of us go away sorrowful because the price seems too high.

This was well expressed by the English poet Sidney Royse Lysaght in a poem which he called "The Penalty of Love." It provides a fitting conclusion to this discussion:

> *If love should count you worthy, and should deign*
> *One day to seek your door and be your guest,*
> *Pause! ere you draw the bolt and bid him rest,*
> *If in your old content you would remain,*
> *For not alone he enters; in his train*
> *Are angels of the mist, the lonely guest,*
> *Dreams of the unfulfilled and unpossessed,*
> *And sorrow, and Life's immemorial pain.*
>
> *He wakes desires you never may forget,*
> *He shows you stars you never saw before,*
> *He makes you share with him, for evermore,*
> *The burden of the world's divine regret.*
> *How wise you were to open not! And yet,*
> *How poor if you should turn him from the door!*

EPILOGUE

Toward Peace on Earth

In this book I have concentrated almost exclusively on the function of anger in one limited, though very important, area of human life—in close relationships. Indeed, I have confined the discussion to the marriage relationship, although most of what I have said would apply equally to parent and child, to siblings, and to other close and continuing interactions between individuals.

However, there are wider fields of human relationship in which anger is an issue and to which much that I have said would not be applicable. Of these I cannot speak with any kind of authority, although I have listed in the bibliography a few sources which I have investigated.

In these closing words I would like to go a little further. Having gained a good deal of experience of the roles of anger in close relationships, I have inevitably, from time to time, looked over the fence of the limited area I was investigating and wondered how far what I was learning might also have some validity "out there."

I was particularly intrigued in my reading of Kenneth E.

Moyer's book *The Physiology of Hostility*, to which I owe such a debt of gratitude, to find that he also, in a highly technical work on a scientific topic, found himself confronted with the wider implications of his studies.

> Man's capacity for total world destruction is a constant threat that makes peace between nations essential to the survival of the species. If peace cannot be maintained, other problems are of little importance. How an understanding of the physiology of aggressive behavior will reduce international conflict is not yet clear. Obviously, wars are the result of a complex of interacting social, political, economic, and other factors, forces that ultimately act on individuals. Thus, any increase in our understanding and control of human behavior may contribute to our understanding and control of the behavior of nations.
>
> World peace, however, involves more than the absence of conflict among nations. A peaceful world must include a general reduction in man's hostility to man in all human interactions. Individual hostile behavior must be reduced if man is to achieve his potential for a quality life. The argument that some hostility is of value, or may be, is irrelevant. Men of introspection must agree that much of their anger and irritability is neither rational nor of value. Control of individual irascibility will contribute to world peace, broadly defined, and an understanding of the physiological substrates of that behavior has much to contribute to such control.[1]

In the course of his remarks, Moyer quotes a short passage from Anthony Storr's book on *Human Aggression*:

> If stability in world affairs is ever to be achieved, the psychological point of view deserves equal consideration with the political, economic, and other aspects. The study of human aggression and its control is, therefore, relevant to the problem of war although alone, it cannot possibly provide a complete answer.[2]

Unfortunately, we seem to be living in an era when the possibilities of aggression developing between both individuals and groups appear to be widespread and steadily increasing. Unprecedented opportunities for communication and travel, while they could theoretically spread good will, frequently have the opposite effect by enabling persons and groups of hostile intent to be in direct contact with each other. Moreover, the mass media, accurately judging that sensational news is popular, tend to report more instances of bad behavior than of good behavior, and thereby convey the impression that resort to violence is a commonplace way of reacting to differences and disagreements. This is further encouraged by the ease with which access can be gained to deadly weapons. All these are highly disturbing elements in today's world.

Yet there is evidence that we are not bound to be influenced by these trends. Some American cities have for some years been considered unsafe at night, and not without reason. Yet as I write these words, a news item has just come through about the crime rate in Japan. One reference is to Tokyo, now the largest city in the world. It is reported that in the last year for which records were available, there had been just *one* street murder in Tokyo! It seems, therefore, that there must exist ways and means by which we could reduce the present tendency to resort to violence—among both individuals and groups.

Better Marriages, Better Families, Better Communities

I am in no way qualified to make recommendations about civic and national programs to curb aggressive behavior. But surely an important starting point would be to offer families better ways of managing the anger that inevitably develops in close relationships. After all, most people in the world spend their impressionable years, and most of their later years for that matter, in some kind of family. Within the family structure they learn to cooperate, or not to cooperate, with others. Ample evidence exists that children deprived of love and emotional security tend to go out into the adult world with chips on their shoulders, often to swell the ranks of criminals. There is also ample evidence, as a result of recent studies of family violence, that parents who "batter" their children, and each other, prove over and over again to have been themselves physically abused in childhood.

There can be few husbands and wives, or parents and children, who would deliberately choose to live in an atmosphere of mutual aggression if they had the alternative choice of living together in peace and harmony. Why then does all the bickering and hassling and battering go on? Because these unhappy people know of no better way; because no one has demonstrated to them, or trained them to understand, that their anger could be managed creatively and that they could live together in a loving and caring atmosphere in which they would give each other mutual support. As a TV personality said recently, "Have you ever heard of a boy raised in a loving and happy family who suddenly, at the age of eighteen, decided to become a robber and a rapist?"

During the years in which Vera and I have been working with couples, I have often noticed how, after an experience of marriage enrichment and a commitment to ongoing growth, parents will report that their children are much more pleasant to live with. I recall one mother who said, with genuine surprise, "I can't figure it out, but since we started working seriously on our marriage, Johnny has been so pleasant. He had been giving us a lot of trouble, but that's all over now."

I had no difficulty in figuring it out. Children have an inner identification with both of their parents, and when those parents are in conflict or estranged, their conflict becomes internalized in the children and makes them angry, insecure, and frustrated—a condition often reflected in their disorderly behavior. But when they see their parents radiating affection and tenderness toward each other, their anxiety is relieved, and they feel inwardly secure and happy. Often after we have visited in the homes of couples who have been into marriage enrichment for several years, I have remarked, "What delightful children are produced by truly happy marriages!"

If we could experience a whole generation of harmonious

and loving families, we would see the benefits reflected in every section of the community and of the nation. We would surely witness a vast improvement in physical and mental health; a startling reduction in delinquency and crime, in personality disorder and social pathology, in addiction to alcohol and drugs; a marked improvement in student behavior in schools, in responsibility and productivity in the work place, in public safety in our cities.

But how can we possibly hope to improve the quality of human relationships in the community unless we first improve the families that make up the community? And how can we produce healthy and happy families unless we first have healthy and happy marriages?

Consider the billions of dollars we are now spending to take care of the fallout from non-functioning families, and the armies of skilled professionals who are seeking to put right in family relationships what should never have been allowed to go wrong! If we could transfer some of that money and some of these dedicated people to the task of developing programs to train members of families not yet in trouble to achieve the kinds of relationships that would keep them out of trouble, how much more would we gain in return for what we had spent?

Some dismiss such an idea by saying that people would never act preventively. That was once true of insurance, but now most people have it. That was once true of medical and dental checkups, but now they are considered routine. If preventive services to families were really made available, while there might be a slow response at first, it would so obviously have good results that the idea would surely catch on in time.

Our business enterprises are pretty good at convincing people that their products can enhance their lives, and they soon have plenty of takers. If I were to invent a gadget that would save busy housewives five minutes a day, in no time they'd all be buying one. And if this same process could convince families that there is a way of making anger work to increase happiness together at home, would they not accept it?

Yes, it will all take time. But the important thing is that we make a real start. It may take long years for us to make our world a really safe place for people to live together in harmony and peace. But most of the benefits we are now enjoying are ours because determined pioneers in the past saw the need for change and got started, often in spite of the indifference and skepticism of the people around them. Surely we owe it to them, to ourselves, to our children, and to future generations to get to work on this vital task.

Notes

Chapter 1

[1]Kenneth E. Moyer, *The Physiology of Hostility* (Chicago: Markham, 1971), p. 5.
[2]Ibid., p. 6.
[3]Ibid.
[4]Ibid., pp. 15–16.
[5]Daniel Coleman, *Psychology Today* (February, 1981): 46.
[6]David H. Burns, *Psychology Today* (November, 1980): 41.

Chapter 2

[1]Moyer, *Physiology*, p. 5.
[2]Erich Fromm, *The Anatomy of Human Destructiveness* (Greenwich, Conn.: Fawcett, 1973), p. 39.
[3]M. F. Ashley Montagu, *On Being Human* (New York: Hawthorn, 1966), p. 44.
[4]Moyer, *Physiology*, pp. 7–8.
[5]Ibid,. p. 23.

Chapter 5

[1]Jane Howard, *Please Touch* (New York: Dell, 1970), p. 54.
[2]Murray A. Straus and Gerald T. Hotaling, *The Social Causes of Husband-Wife Violence* (Minneapolis: University of Minnesota Press, 1980), p. 270.
[3]Israel Charney, *Marital Love and Hate* (New York: Macmillan, 1972), p. 84.

Epilogue

[1]Moyer, *Physiology*.
[2]Anthony Storr, *Human Aggression* (New York: Allen Lane, 1968), p. 369

APPENDIX

Resources for Couples

Most of the suggestions I have made in this book can be acted on directly by any couple who are ready to get to work on their relationship. In addition, I want to add here some further sources of information and help.

Couples who want to improve their communication skills by taking short courses which are now available can approach two organizations which I can confidently recommend. They are

Interpersonal Communication Programs, Inc.,
1925 Nicollet
Minneapolis, Minnesota 55403

and the

Institute for the Development of Emotional and
Life Skills, Inc. (IDEALS)
P.O. Box 391
Pennsylvania State University
University Park, Pennsylvania 16801

In the wider field of marriage enrichment, the best source of information is the

Association of Couples for Marriage Enrichment
(ACME)
P.O. Box 10596
459 South Church Street
Winston-Salem, N.C. 27108

This is the organization Vera and I established in 1973. It is now an international association of married couples whose members are willing "to work for better marriages, beginning with their own." Membership is open to married couples, and associate membership to others; all receive a monthly newsletter. ACME has member couples in all the states, most of the Canadian provinces, and in other countries across the world. Affiliated organizations exist in Australia, Britain, and South Africa. ACME also serves as the coordinator for the Council of Affiliated Marriage Enrichment Organizations (CAMEO), which represents about twenty-five North American organizations providing marriage enrichment programs on a *national* basis. Most of the religious denominations now provide programs in marriage enrichment, and it has been estimated that more than one-and-a-half million couples have participated in marriage enrichment retreats or other events. This is a new field in which interest is growing rapidly.

Vera and I have now coauthored three books about marriage enrichment:

We Can Have Better Marriages, If We Really Want Them (Abingdon, 1974)
Marriage Enrichment in the Church (Broadman, 1976)
How To Have a Happy Marriage (Abingdon, 1977).

Also, I have written:
Close Companions: The Marriage Enrichment Handbook (Crossroad, 1982).

Bibliography

Over a period of years, I have read a great deal of material on the subject of anger. I feel no need here to list articles and other such sources, and have confined this list to published books which have come to my notice. They will enable any reader to explore the subject further.

Ardrey, R. *The Territorial Imperative*. New York: Atheneum, 1966.

Augsburger, David W. *The Love Fight*. Scottdale, Penna.: Herald Press, 1975.

Bach, George R., and Goldberg, Herb. *Creative Aggression: The Art of Assertive Living*. New York: Doubleday, 1974.

Bach, George R., and Wyden, Peter. *The Intimate Enemy: How To Fight Fair in Love and Marriage*. New York: Morrow, 1970.

Bergler, Edmund. *Conflict In Marriage*. England: Windmill Press, 1951.

Berkowitz, L. *Aggression: A Social Psychological Analysis*. New York: McGraw-Hill, 1962.

Bry, Adelaide. *How To Get Angry Without Feeling Guilty*. New York: Signet Paperback, 1972.

Buss, A. *The Psychology of Aggression*. New York: Wiley, 1961.

Charney, Israel. *Marital Love and Hate*. New York: Macmillan, 1972.

Clemente, C. V., and Lindsley, D. B., eds. *Aggression and Defense: Neural Mechanisms and Social Patterns*. Los Angeles: University of California Press, 1967.

Coser, Lewis A. *The Functions of Social Conflict*. New York: Free Press, 1956.

Dicks, H. V. *Marital Tensions*. New York: Basic Books, 1968.

Eisenstein, V. W., ed. *Neurotic Interaction in Marriage*. New York: Basic Books, 1965.

Freud, Sigmund. *The Psychopathology of Everyday Life*. Standard Edition, Vol. 6. New York: Macmillan, 1960.

Fromm, Erich. *The Anatomy of Human Destructiveness*. Greenwich, Conn.: Fawcett, 1973.

Fromm, Erich. *The Heart of Man: Its Genius for Good and Evil*. New York: Harper, 1964.

Garattini, S., and Sigg, E. B., eds. *Aggressive Behavior*. New York: Wiley, 1969.

Gelles, Richard J. *The Violent Home: A Study of Physical Aggression Between Husbands and Wives*. Beverly Hill, Ca.: Sage Publications, 1972.

Houck, Paul A. *Overcoming Frustration and Anger*. Philadelphia: Westminster Press, 1974.

Howard, Jane. *Please Touch*. New York: Dell, 1970.

Lorenz, Konrad. *On Aggression*. New York: Bantam Books, 1966.

Mace, David and Vera. *We Can Have Better Marriages*. Nashville: Abingdon Press, 1974.

Mace, David and Vera. *How To Have a Happy Marriage*. Nashville: Abingdon Press, 1977.

Madour, Leo. *Anger: How To Recognize and Cope With It*. New York: Scribner, 1972.

Mark, V. H., and Ervin, F. R. *Violence and the Brain*. New York: Harper and Row, 1970.

Menninger, Karl. *Love Against Hate*. New York: Harcourt Brace, 1942.

Moyer, Kenneth E. *The Physiology of Hostility*. Chicago: Markham, 1971.

Montagu, M. F. Ashley. *Man and Aggression*. London: Oxford University Press, 1968.

Montagu, M. F. Ashley. *On Being Human*. New York: Hawthorn, 1966.

Plattner, Paul. *Conflict and Understanding in Marriage*. Richmond, Va.: John Knox Press, 1970.

Raush, Harold L.; Barry, William A.; Hertel, Richard K.; Swain, Mary Ann. *Communication, Conflict, and Marriage: Explorations in the Theory and Study of Intimate Relationships*. San Francisco: Jossey-Bass, 1974.

Rubin, Theodore Isaac. *The Angry Book*. New York: Collier, 1969.

Saul, L. J. *The Hostile Mind: The Sources and Consequences of Rage and Hate*. New York: Random House, 1956.

Scanzoni, John. *Sexual Bargaining*. Englewood Cliffs, N.J.: Prentice-Hall, 1972.

Scott, J.P.. *Just Aggression*. Chicago: University of Chicago Press, 1958.

Scott, J.P. and Eleftheriou, B. E., eds. *The Physiology of Fighting and Defeat*. Chicago: University of Chicago Press, 1971.

Southard, Samuel. *Anger in Love*. Philadelphia: Westminster Press, 1973.

Storr, Anthony. *Human Aggression*. New York: Allen Lane, 1968.

Straus, Murray A., and Hotaling, Gerald T. *The Social Causes of Husband-Wife Violence*. Minneapolis: University of Minnesota Press, 1980.

Tournier, Paul. *The Violence Within*. New York: Harper and Row, 1978.

Winter, Gibson. *Love and Conflict: New Patterns in Family Life*. New York: Doubleday, 1961.